from Your Friends at The MAILBOX®

MORE Classroom Adventures
Center-Based
Themes for Early Childhood

Written by
Karen V. Jones

Edited by
Ada Goren
Jan Trautman

Illustrated by
Pam Crane, Teresa R. Davidson,
Theresa Lewis Goode,
Sheila Krill, Rob Mayworth,
Kimberly Richard, Greg D. Rieves,
Rebecca Saunders, Barry Slate

Cover designed by
Kimberly Richard

www.themailbox.com

©2000 by THE EDUCATION CENTER, INC.
All rights reserved.
ISBN# 1-56234-354-8

Manufactured in the United States
10 9 8 7 6 5 4 3 2 1

Table of Contents

Introduction

What's the key to a young child's academic success? It's an immersion into science, language, and math all wrapped up in a wonderful package called *play!* Play is a child's work. It's the means by which a child makes discoveries and builds knowledge of the world around him. It's a safe and natural way for him to try out new roles, experiment with objects, utilize his senses, and express his creativity. Where does the teacher fit into all this? He or she is a facilitator, readying the environment, providing materials, and opening up possibilities for new explorations along the way.

With that theory in mind, this book strives to provide you with a myriad of developmentally appropriate ideas that have been field-tested by hundreds of inquisitive youngsters just like the ones you teach! Each unit in *More Classroom Adventures* is a map that will take your class on a journey without leaving your school. You'll find ideas for your favorite centers that will help you transform your classroom into an exciting environment just full of possibilities for learning! There's enough creative fuel stored in these pages to take you from coast to coast or just around the corner. All it takes is a little planning and a whole lot of imagination!

And while your students are exploring, they'll be developing important skills, which you'll see listed next to each and every center area. You'll also find activities to get parents involved and an open reproducible at the end of each unit, so you can share with them the highlights of your trips.

So pick a destination and pack your bags. And remember that the most important thing—the thing that will have children bounding into your room each day with wide smiles, the thing that will motivate you to get to school early, stay late, or make that extra trip to the discount store, the thing that everyone loves—is to have FUN!

3

Packing Your Bags

There are a few basics that you'll want to bring along regardless of the class-room adventure you choose. Having the following materials packed and ready to go will give you more time to enjoy the journey.

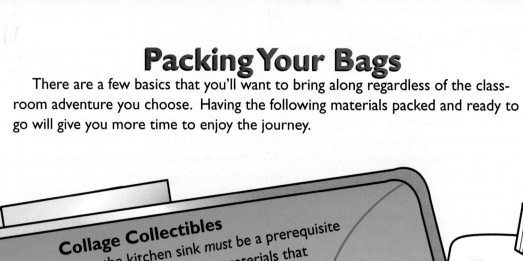

Collage Collectibles

Recycling everything but the kitchen sink *must* be a prerequisite to great teaching! Create categories of collage materials that complement each other and provide a variety of interest in texture and color. You may need to prepare small pieces of some materials for easy handling and cutting, but allow plenty of room for self-expression and exploration.

Begin with:
colored cellophane cut into strips or squares; assorted tissue paper; crepe paper streamers; curling ribbon; Mylar® scraps; aluminum foil; shredded or crinkled gift packaging; wrapping paper; sequins; buttons; dyed macaroni; foil confetti; Styrofoam® peanuts; shredded computer paper; Easter grass; popcorn kernels; dried beans; birdseed; fabric scraps; wallpaper squares; bits of yarn, lace, and rickrack; chenille stems…*and add anything else you can find!*

"Plue"

This is a mixture of one part white school paste and one part white school glue. It can be tinted any color with a touch of tempera. Stir until it almost resembles frosting. It will ad-here nearly anything to any surface, dry hard, and wash off in a jiffy. It also s-t-r-e-t-c-h-e-s your glue budget and keeps indefinitely in the fridge.

Sensory-Table Utensils

Rarely filled with *only* sand or water, the sensory tables in each unit provide experiences rich with science, math, and language…not to mention socialization! Having some of the following utensils on hand will allow you to adapt the activities and challenge each child according to her developmental ability.

Try these kitchen utensils:
slotted spoons, ladles, spatulas, wooden spoons, ice-cream scoops, pasta forks, potato mashers, tongs, colanders, measuring cups, funnels, strainers, turkey basters, mixing bowls, muffin tins, cake pans
…*and keep your eye out for other great tools to use!*

ADMIT ONE

Glittery Stuff

Whether it's in artwork, play dough, or water tables, a pinch of glitter makes the ordinary extraordinary! To make glitter go twice as far, add one part table salt to one part glitter. Mix a variety of colors ahead of time and store them in plastic bags or airtight containers.

Foil confetti, available in the party section of craft and toy stores, is a must-have on your supply list. It's fun to use, easy to clean up, and costs just a penny a pinch!

Tempera Paint

Premix one part liquid dish detergent into two parts tempera paint to make cleanup easier. Store the paint in gallon jugs or pour it back into detergent bottles. You'll have a rainbow at your fingertips!

Homemade "Watery-colors"

Stir a few drops of food coloring into a bowl of water. Add a splash of vinegar. Make a variety of colors and store them in airtight containers. This will keep indefinitely!

Sugar Chalk

This is like paint on a stick! Add one part sugar to four parts very hot water and drop in sticks of colored sidewalk chalk. Wait for about five minutes or until all the fizzing stops. Pull the chalk out of the sugar water and draw with it immediately. Or let the chalk dry and then store it in a plastic bag. When you're ready to use it, dunk it into plain water first; then draw.

Note: Do _not_ use this on chalkboards. Use on paper only.

Monoprints

When you want children to paint BIG and w-i-d-e on the surfaces of tables, trays, or easels instead of directly on paper, use this technique to send a piece of artwork home. Simply press a piece of paper on part of the design, rub, and then peel it off. Ta da!

The Best Birthday Party Ever!

That's right—everybody can have a birthday at the same time! Why not? We're *all* one day older! So let's go to a special party where every birthday child will be celebrated for being just who he or she is!

ADMIT ONE

ADMIT ONE

Getting Ready to Go!

You'll need a supply of birthday goodies to make this celebration special. Check out the lists on page 7; then gather what you'll need according to the centers you choose. Use the ideas below to add to the party atmosphere.

Decorate!

Cover the children's work tables with store-bought birthday-themed tablecloths, or have your youngsters make them. To make one, purchase a solid-colored cloth tablecloth and some water-based fabric paint. Invite each little reveler to make a paint handprint on the cloth for a personalized, festive touch! In addition, hang some crepe paper streamers from the ceiling. To top it all off, blow up a balloon for each child and use a permanent marker to write the child's name and age on it. For safety, hang the balloons out of children's reach.

A Birthday Board

Make a festive bulletin board to show off all the birthday cards and other writings and drawings your youngsters create during this unit. Cover the background of the board with birthday wrapping paper. Add a bouquet of uninflated Mylar® balloons on one side. Then use gift bows and pushpins to attach children's work to the board.

Pictures, Please

You'll need photos for some of the centers in this unit. Send home a note asking parents to supply photos of their children for "Party Portraits" on page 8 and photos from their children's previous birthdays for "A Class Birthday Album" on page 9.

Party Supplies

Choose from the center ideas on pages 8–13. Here's a handy list of the supplies you'll need to complete each one.

Art Area

Party Hats: 12" x 18" construction paper, markers, collage materials, glue, crepe paper or cellophane streamers, stapler
"Krazy" Kazoos: toilet tissue rolls; markers, glitter pens, and/or stickers; waxed paper; rubber bands
Frosting for the Fun of It!: pastry bags and tips, frosting, Styrofoam® plates or bowls, unfrosted cupcakes (optional)
Party Portraits: photos of students, clear Con-Tact® paper, construction paper, confetti, ribbon, star stickers, markers

Reading Center

A Class Birthday Album: photos from students' previous birthdays, construction paper, markers, stapler or other binding

Sensory Tables and Tubs

Make a Wish!: foil confetti, ladles, metal bowls
Some Like Their Wishes Dry...: paper confetti, scoops, funnels, baskets, large mixing bowls
Birthday Balloons: transparent balloons, birthday candles, confetti, hand soap
The More Batter, the Better!: boxes of cornstarch, vanilla extract, brown tempera paint or red and green food coloring, mixing bowls, measuring cups, wooden spoons, rubber spatulas, kitchen towels, electric hand mixer with cord removed (optional)

Writing Center

A Whimsical Wish Story: bulletin board paper, markers, crayons
You're Invited!: paper, envelopes, crayons, stickers, rubber stamps, ink pads

Dramatic-Play Center

Smile and Say "Chee-e-e-e-ze!": old or toy cameras, disposable cameras
Let's Bake a Cake!: baking utensils, cake pans, cupcake liners and tins, empty boxes of cake mix, empty frosting containers, birthday candles, pictures of cakes from magazines and cookbooks

Music and Movement

Strike Up the Band!: rhythm instruments, crepe paper streamers, recording of marching band music

Science Center

Does Everything Have a Birthday?: poster board, glue sticks, pictures of living and nonliving things from magazines

Block Area

Wrapping It Up: colored comics, wrapping paper, scissors, clear or masking tape
Blocks in a Box: sturdy cardboard boxes, Con-Tact® paper or gift wrap

Party Hats

For each child, fold a sheet of 12" x 18" construction paper as illustrated in Step 1. Assist each child in writing her name on the rim of her hat with a bold marker; then let the decorating begin! Offer a concoction of confetti, sequins, pom-poms or colored cotton balls, crinkled gift wrap stuffing, plastic Easter grass, dyed pasta shapes, star stickers, and anything else you can think of! Top off each hat with a few crepe paper or cellophane streamers and then staple the hat together as shown in Step 2. Let the party begin!

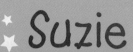

Step 1

Step 2

"Krazy" Kazoos

Make a little party music with these ever-popular instruments that make use of those abundant toilet tissue rolls! Encourage each artist to decorate a cardboard roll with her choice of markers, glitter pens, and/or stickers. Then use a rubber band to secure a square of waxed paper over one end of each roll. You may need to demonstrate the technique of playing such an unusual instrument, so hum a few bars yourself!

Frosting for the Fun of It!

How often do youngsters get to try their hands at cake decorating? They'll be quick to master this craft when you supply the tools of the trade! Purchase a few real pastry bags with a variety of tips. Then whip up a batch of buttercream frosting or simply combine enough powdered sugar and shortening to create a stiff but squeezable frosting. Add some food coloring, of course! Set out some "cakes" made from upside-down Styrofoam® plates or bowls. Then partially fill each pastry bag (fitted with a tip) with frosting. If desired, have children decorate real cupcakes instead! Your cake designers will have a ball!

Party Portraits

Photos of the birthday child are a must! Ask parents to send in photos, or take a photo of each child at school. For each youngster, cut a 9" x 12" piece of clear Con-Tact® paper and a 9" x 12" frame from construction paper. Affix the paper frame to the Con-Tact paper. With the sticky side of the Con-Tact paper facing up, have each child stick his photo in the center of his paper frame. Have him decorate the clear area with birthday confetti, ribbon, and star stickers; then have him add marker decorations to the paper frame if he likes. If desired, have each child use a marker to write his name and age on the frame. Display the portraits in your classroom throughout the unit; then send them home to become treasured keepsakes.

A Class Birthday Album

Create a class birthday album with special photos of your students' birthdays past (see "Pictures, Please" on page 6). Label each page with the child's name and age at the time of the picture. Little ones will love looking at pictures of themselves and classmates and they'll be practicing their numbers, too!

Class Birthdays

Jason   Age 5

A Bounty of Birthday Books

Stock your reading center with these celebration stories!

Happy Birthday, Jesse Bear!
By Nancy White Carlstrom
Simon & Schuster Children's Division

It's My Birthday
By Helen Oxenbury
Candlewick Press

Ask Mr. Bear
By Marjorie Flack
Aladdin Paperbacks

Happy Birthday, Dear Duck
By Eve Bunting
Houghton Mifflin Company

Birthday Monsters!
By Sandra Boynton
Workman Publishing Company

Dramatic-Play Center

Language development
Cooperative skills
Word/picture association
Socialization

Smile and Say "Chee-e-e-e-ze!"

Where there's a party, there's a camera! So stock up on a variety of used or toy cameras for pretend photo shoots. Sneak a couple of real disposable cameras into this center, and you'll be treated to some shots of life from a child's perspective! What fun you'll all have when the film is developed!

Let's Bake a Cake!

Have a variety of props on hand to help your little bakers mix up some birthday treats. Include rubber spatulas, egg beaters, mixing bowls, cupcake liners and tins, and cake pans. Also provide empty cake mix boxes, empty frosting containers, and some birthday candles, as well as some laminated pictures of cakes cut from magazines or old cookbooks.

Sensory Tables and Tubs

Tactile exploration
Analytical thinking
Language development
Imaginative play

Make a Wish!

Who can resist a tub full of colorful confetti? Grab a few bags of foil confetti from the party section of your local craft store and sprinkle it by the handful into a tub of water. Add a couple of ladles for stirring and some metal bowls to reflect those special birthday wishes. When you're done with this center, drain and dry the confetti for future use.

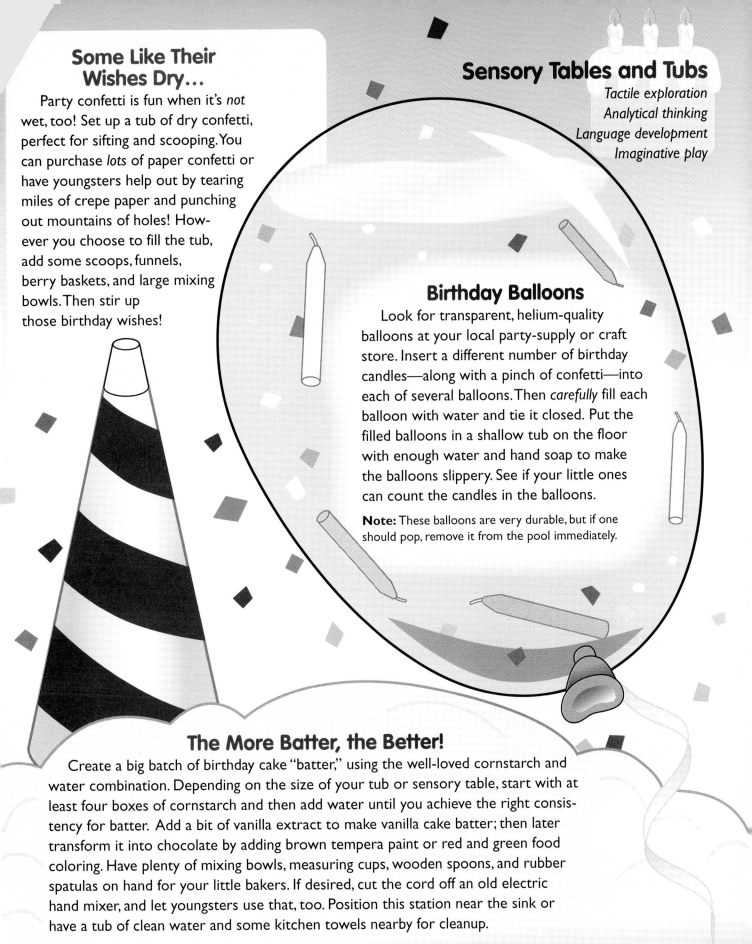

Some Like Their Wishes Dry…

Party confetti is fun when it's *not* wet, too! Set up a tub of dry confetti, perfect for sifting and scooping. You can purchase *lots* of paper confetti or have youngsters help out by tearing miles of crepe paper and punching out mountains of holes! However you choose to fill the tub, add some scoops, funnels, berry baskets, and large mixing bowls. Then stir up those birthday wishes!

Birthday Balloons

Look for transparent, helium-quality balloons at your local party-supply or craft store. Insert a different number of birthday candles—along with a pinch of confetti—into each of several balloons. Then *carefully* fill each balloon with water and tie it closed. Put the filled balloons in a shallow tub on the floor with enough water and hand soap to make the balloons slippery. See if your little ones can count the candles in the balloons.

Note: These balloons are very durable, but if one should pop, remove it from the pool immediately.

The More Batter, the Better!

Create a big batch of birthday cake "batter," using the well-loved cornstarch and water combination. Depending on the size of your tub or sensory table, start with at least four boxes of cornstarch and then add water until you achieve the right consistency for batter. Add a bit of vanilla extract to make vanilla cake batter; then later transform it into chocolate by adding brown tempera paint or red and green food coloring. Have plenty of mixing bowls, measuring cups, wooden spoons, and rubber spatulas on hand for your little bakers. If desired, cut the cord off an old electric hand mixer, and let youngsters use that, too. Position this station near the sink or have a tub of clean water and some kitchen towels nearby for cleanup.

Writing Center

Language development
Creative thinking
Writing skills
Listening skills

A Whimsical Wish Story

Turn happy thoughts and children's fancies into one great big birthday wish story! Record each child's birthday wish on a long sheet of bulletin board paper. Remember—nothing is too preposterous for a preschooler! Invite little ones to illustrate the story if they wish! Then hang it for all to see.

You're Invited!

Set up a card-making center with shoeboxes full of colorful paper, envelopes, crayons, stickers, and rubber stamps. Creating invitations is as much fun as receiving them! Write out younger children's dictation or post a list of birthday-related words for older students to copy. Or let them invent some words of their own! If desired, have youngsters use this center to create invitations to a class birthday celebration (see "Family Focus" on page 14).

Science Center

Analytical thinking
Concepts of time
Verbal skills
Exploration of living and nonliving things

Does Everything Have a Birthday?

Having birthdays is a natural part of life. It means you're getting older. But does everything age? Invite children to create a poster in your science center. Put out a sheet of poster board, glue sticks, and pictures cut from magazines. Have youngsters glue pictures onto the poster board until it's full. Then discuss the pictures of people, animals, and plants that *do* grow and the pictures of nonliving objects that *don't*.

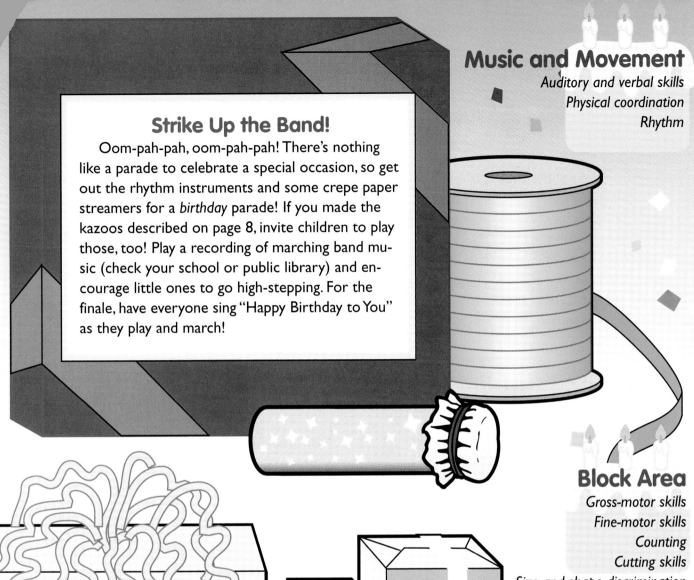

Strike Up the Band!

Oom-pah-pah, oom-pah-pah! There's nothing like a parade to celebrate a special occasion, so get out the rhythm instruments and some crepe paper streamers for a *birthday* parade! If you made the kazoos described on page 8, invite children to play those, too! Play a recording of marching band music (check your school or public library) and encourage little ones to go high-stepping. For the finale, have everyone sing "Happy Birthday to You" as they play and march!

Block Area
Gross-motor skills
Fine-motor skills
Counting
Cutting skills
Size and shape discrimination
Socialization

Wrapping It Up

All children love to wrap and unwrap presents, but they usually get to do it only a few times a year. At this wrapping center, they can do it every day! Collect colorful comics and oodles of recycled wrapping paper (any season will do). Provide scissors and *lots* of clear or masking tape. Invite your gift wrappers to pick out different sizes and shapes of blocks to wrap. A simple demonstration from you is all they'll need to get started.

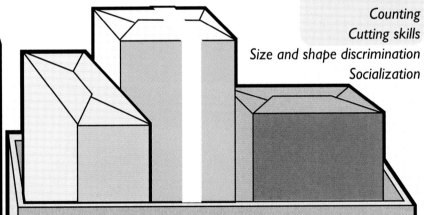

Blocks in a Box

Don't you just love it when you receive a present in the mail? But packing those presents for shipping can be quite a challenge sometimes! Encourage your youngsters to take the challenge with this center idea. Provide a supply of sturdy boxes in assorted sizes. Cover a variety of blocks with colorful Con-Tact® paper or gift wrap. Then ask youngsters to find creative ways to pack the "presents" into the boxes for shipping.

Tips for an Extended Stay

Once your classroom centers are set for a birthday theme, try these ideas for a group project, outdoor fun, and family involvement. Party on!

All Together Now

Make your collaborative birthday celebration really special by having your little ones *give* the presents! Work together to prepare and decorate a batch of birthday cupcakes. Then surprise another class by delivering them at snacktime or just after lunch. Now they can celebrate their special, one-day-older birthdays, too!

Family Focus

Hooray! It's time for the party! Invite parents to join your class for a super-duper celebration! Make the menu and the activities silly. Bake upside-down cupcakes or concoct upside-down sundaes. Play Pin the Tail on the Elephant. Have a wrapping or an unwrapping race. Enjoy the party and one another on this extra-ordinary day!

Out 'n' About

Party favors are always fun, especially when they're part of an outdoor treasure hunt! Purchase a class supply of minibottles of bubbles. Hide the bottles on your playground for little ones to find and enjoy. As a variation, place each bottle in a tiny gift bag and label the bag with a child's name. Challenge each youngster to find her personalized party favor. Then blow some birthday bubbles—and don't forget to make wishes!

Highlights of Our Trip
The Best Birthday Party Ever!

This really was the best party ever because it was *everybody's* birthday! To find out about the festivities, read on!

All Around Our Neighborhood

Welcome, neighbor...come on in and stay a while! During this down-home adventure, children will discover that they are part of a very special community—in their own school and in the big world beyond! There are people and places common to everyone, wherever you live. Hey, it really *is* a small world after all!

ADMIT ONE

Getting Ready to Go!

Prepare for this trip around the block and back by gathering the supplies you'll need. Check the lists on page 17; then collect what you'll need based upon the centers you choose. You may need help collecting a few items, so read on....

ADMIT ONE

So, Who *Are* the People in the Neighborhood?

Gather a variety of dress-up clothing, including occupational uniforms, aprons, and hats from folks your little ones might encounter in the neighborhood. This may take some time, but it will be well worth it. And people *like* to share! While you're at it, you may want to invite some of your friendly donors to make a visit to your class and introduce themselves!

Box Houses

Scavenge a few large appliance boxes to serve as a miniature neighborhood for the center described in "A Neighborhood Renovation" on page 23. Use a utility knife (when children aren't around) to cut windows and doors from the boxes so that each one resembles a house.

Don't Toss the Junk Mail— or the Trash!

Ask parents to help you collect some items you'll need for some of the centers in this unit. You're going to need *lots* of mail—any kind—for "Mail's Here!" on page 21. And you'll also need clean recyclable materials—such as plastic bottles, aluminum cans, and newspaper—for the "Recycling Zone" activity on page 23. Assure parents that you'll properly recycle the items after using them in your classroom.

Neighborhood Needs

Choose from the center ideas on pages 18–23. Here's a handy
list of the supplies you'll need to prepare each one.

Art Area

Hi, Neighbor!: large sheets
of construction paper, white slide
frames or white construction paper frames,
glue, crayons or markers
Neighborhood Paintings: assorted colors of tempera
paint (including multicultural skin tones), easel paper, paintbrushes
A Small World: small Styrofoam® balls, paintbrushes, squares of blue and
green tissue paper, diluted glue or liquid starch, pipe cleaners, newspaper
The Neighborhood Kids: gingerbread boy and girl cookie cutters, air-drying modeling
compound, collage materials

Reading Center

We Love the Library!: small pencils, index cards,
marker, library card pockets (optional)

Science Center

Fingerprints: stamp pads, index cards, magnifying
glasses, chart with students' names

Dramatic-Play Center

The Friendliest Grocery in Town!: nonperishable groceries, grocery bags, play money, toy
cash register, adding machine, magazine rack, magazines, paper, crayons, aprons, and a price
gun borrowed from a grocery store (optional)
At the Sweet Shop: colorful pom-poms or Ping-Pong® balls, plastic scoops, small zippered
plastic bags or paper lunch bags, simple scale

Sensory Tables and Tubs

It's Wash Day!: old clothing, liquid dish
detergent, clothesline, clothespins,
towels, laundry baskets
Tending the Garden: potting soil,
small shovels, flower or vegetable
seeds, silk flowers, potatoes, carrots
Mail's Here!: mail in various sizes and
shapes, canvas tote bags

Block Area

Recycling Zone: clean recyclable
items, recycling bins or large boxes,
marker, work gloves, wagon or
wheelbarrow
A Neighborhood Renovation: box
houses, paintbrushes and rollers, tempera paint and newspaper (optional)

Music and Movement

Around the Block and Back: vinyl tile squares or carpet squares, masking tape, marker, recorded music

Writing Center

Walkin' Through Our Neighborhood: copy paper, career-related clothing and tools, markers or crayons, construction paper or tagboard
Guess Who!: a supply of copy paper and tagboard cut into house shapes, markers, magazines, scissors, glue sticks

Art Area

Creative expression
Cultural awareness/Social studies
Color and shape recognition
Fine-motor skills

Hi, Neighbor!

Not everyone lives in a house—apartments are homes, too! Encourage each of your young artists to make an apartment collage on a large piece of construction paper. Provide each child with several white frames used for slides (available in camera stores) or cut your own small frames from construction paper. A child "builds" her apartment building by gluing the frames all over her paper to resemble windows, then drawing in the friendly faces she sees in her neighborhood.

Neighborhood Paintings

Stock your easel area with tempera paint in an array of colors, including multicultural skin tones. Invite students to think about their neighborhoods and the people who live and work there. Then ask them to describe them through paint. Some may choose to create detailed pictures, others may simply explore color. Remember—it's the process, not the product!

A Small World

Community can mean a group of any size— your family, your class, your school, or even the whole planet! Make this model of the world neighborhood to emphasize that everyone on Earth shares some common experiences. Give each child a small Styrofoam® ball. Have her use a paintbrush and diluted school glue or liquid starch to cover the ball with squares of blue and green tissue paper. Stick half of a pipe cleaner into the ball; then hang it over layers of newspaper to dry. These tiny globes make fun gifts!

The Neighborhood Kids

Bring a group of neighborhood pals to life with this art endeavor! Set out some gingerbread boy and girl cookie cutters, along with an array of buttons, yarn, ribbon, rickrack, and small pom-poms. Have each artist cut a gingerbread boy or girl from air-drying modeling compound. Then have her add collage materials to give her neighborhood kid some personality and style! The art materials will stick in the compound as it dries. Display all these new kids on the block together!

We Love the Library!

Create a replica of your neighborhood library, right in your reading center! Add a few chairs and a small table to the area. Provide small pencils and index cards so little visitors can "check out" books. If desired, purchase some library card pockets from your local teacher supply store and stick them to the backs of some of your classroom books. Make library cards by printing each child's name on a separate index card and then laminating all the cards.

Neighborhood Books

To learn about the many different workers in a neighborhood, check out Our Neighborhood series from Children's Press. These photo-illustrated books depict men and women of different races and cultures working as grocers, dentists, farmers, chefs, police officers, and more. Your youngsters will also enjoy the following selections about neighborhoods and the people who live and work in them.

Franklin's Neighborhood
By Sharon Jennings
Scholastic Trade Books

I Got Community
By Melrose Cooper
Henry Holt and Company, Inc.

Sidewalk Trip
By Patricia Hubbell
HarperCollins Juvenile Books

A Kaleidoscope of Kids
By Emma Damon
Dial Books for Young Readers

Dramatic-Play Center

Creative thinking
Verbal skills
Socialization
Measurement
Money

The Friendliest Grocery in Town!

Stock your dramatic-play area with canned goods, nonperishables, and packaged paper products. Add some grocery bags, play money (either homemade or borrowed from a Monopoly® game), and a toy cash register. Adding machines (either working or not) are also fun! Clear off a table to serve as the checkout stand and set up a magazine rack nearby. Youngsters will enjoy helping make signs and price tags for this center! To give this neighborhood haunt an even more realistic look, ask a local grocery store to lend some aprons and a price gun. Now, will that be paper or plastic?

At the Sweet Shop

Every child enjoys an occasional sweet treat from the candy store! For an imaginative treat that's *almost* as good, try filling a sensory table or a large container with colorful pom-poms and Ping-Pong® balls. Add some plastic scoops and small zippered plastic bags or paper lunch bags. Don't forget a simple scale! Little ones can take turns role-playing the shopkeeper and the buyer.

Sensory Tables and Tubs

Fine-motor skills
Size and shape discrimination
Sorting
Creative thinking
Socialization

It's Wash Day!

Whether it's at home or at the neighborhood Laundromat, everybody has laundry to do. Set up a laundry in a sensory table by supplying real clothes and some soapy suds made with liquid dish detergent. Hang a clothesline nearby, with plenty of towels layered underneath it, and provide a large supply of spring-type clothespins. Better yet, wheel the sensory table outside and invite some neighbors to hang the laundry out on the line!

To extend the feel of a neighborhood Laundromat, stack clean, dry clothes on a nearby table. Set out a few laundry baskets and let the sorting and folding begin!

Mail's Here!

It happens six days a week. The trusty mail carrier arrives with letters and packages for everyone in the neighborhood. But what a job to sort it all out! Fill a sensory table with all sizes and shapes of mail—postcards, small envelopes, business envelopes, mailing envelopes, small boxes, magazines, catalogs, and fliers. Invite youngsters to role-play postal workers and sort the mail into several canvas "mailbags."

Tending the Garden

Hey, neighbor! Doing a little yard work today? All the neighbors will want to visit this gardening center! Fill a sensory table or small wading pool with fresh potting soil. Toss in a few small shovels and provide real flower or vegetable seeds for young gardeners to sprinkle into the soil. (Keep in mind that these may not grow due to continuous digging.) For instant results, have an array of silk flowers for youngsters to plant and replant. Surprise your little ones one day by hiding real carrots and potatoes in the soil. Once youngsters discover the veggies, invite them to help wash, peel, and cook them. Invite all the neighbors to this harvest feast!

Writing Center

Rhythm and patterning in language
Writing skills
Socialization

Walkin' Through Our Neighborhood

Better put on your walking shoes, 'cause we're going door-to-door! Invite each child to contribute a page to a class book about a neighborhood tour. In advance, program a sheet of paper as shown. Make a copy for each child. Place the sheets in your writing center, along with career-related dress-up clothes and tools to jump-start little ones' imaginations. Have each youngster write or dictate about a person he might see in the neighborhood and then add an illustration to his page. Bind all the pages together behind a cover with the title "Walkin' Through Our Neighborhood."

Walkin' through the neighborhood
Who will I see?
I see <u>Mr. Golden</u> waving at me.

This is baby Mia next door.

Guess Who!

For each child, cut a few sheets of copy paper into simple house shapes. Staple a house-shaped tagboard cover to each book and then add the title "Guess Who's in My Neighborhood!" Invite each child to add an illustration to each page or to glue on a magazine picture. Write her dictation on each page as she names the neighbor.

Science Center

Analytical thinking
Visual discrimination
Name recognition

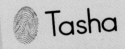

Tasha

David

Fingerprints

Every neighbor is unique—from fingertip to fingertip! Invite the scientists in your classroom neighborhood to study fingerprints in your science center. Set out stamp pads, index cards, and magnifying glasses. Have a child make a few fingerprints on a card and then examine them closely. Can she see special designs? Hang a chart of students' names on a wall and then invite each youngster to make a fingerprint next to her name. Have her use a magnifying glass to detect similarities and differences between her own and her classmates' prints.

Recycling Zone

Every good neighbor recycles, so transform your block area into a recycling center! Borrow some recycling bins or simply use a few large boxes. Label each one for a different type of recyclable material, such as plastic, metal, and paper. Ask parents to help you gather a wide variety of recyclables, such as newspaper, plastic milk jugs, and clean aluminum cans (with the edges taped over for safety). Provide work gloves and a wagon or wheelbarrow. Then invite youngsters to transport and sort!

A Neighborhood Renovation

Bring in the appliance boxes you prepared in "Box Houses" on page 16 and create a mini neighborhood right in your own classroom. Add some invisible paint, paintbrushes, and rollers, and set your little neighbors to fixin' up! Or—if the weather is nice—set up the box houses outdoors on a lavish amount of newspaper and use *real* paint! Don't forget the shutters and window boxes!

Music and Movement

Auditory skills
Gross-motor skills
Name recognition
Socialization

Around the Block and Back

As a variation on Musical Chairs, try playing Musical Houses! Gather a vinyl tile square or a carpet square for each child. Label each square with a different child's name and scatter them on the floor to represent houses in the neighborhood. Play some music and invite youngsters to move around the squares in any motion they choose. When you stop the music, they step onto a house. Whose house is it? Wave to your neighbor! They'll love this game because *everybody* wins *all* the time!

Savanah

Tips for an Extended Stay

Once your classroom neighborhood is well established in your centers, try these ideas for a group project, an outdoor adventure, and a family activity.

All Together Now

This project will give new meaning to the term "block party"! Gather a class supply of wood blocks from a local lumber yard, a home improvement center, or a parent's building project. Mix one part school glue with two parts liquid tempera paint. First, have each student paint a wood piece without adding detail. Then have each child transform her painted block of wood into a building. What type of building? How about a house, a fire station, a school, a grocery store, or a library? Depending on your students' skill level, they could paint windows and doors, draw with permanent markers, or glue on construction paper shapes to complete their buildings. Set up all the buildings as a neighborhood, complete with toy cars and trucks. Leave this on display for a while—little ones may decide to add on!

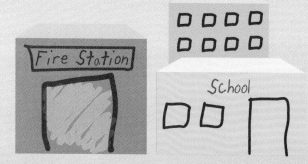

Out 'n' About

If you're headed outdoors, head out on a field trip to one or more of the places in your neighborhood! Find an interesting part of the community that's within walking distance of your school. It could be a grocery store, a library, a gas station, or even a friendly neighbor's house!

Family Focus

Have a *real* block party! Invite families to school to tour the neighborhood centers and see their children's projects and writing. Then enjoy a covered-dish picnic—inside or out. This is a perfect time to show a video highlighting all the great activities your class does, right in their own school neighborhood!

Highlights of Our Trip
All Around the Neighborhood

Just who are the people in our neighborhood? Grocers, postal workers, police officers, beauticians, and librarians…just to name a few! Read below as we introduce you to the people and places we learned about on this trip!

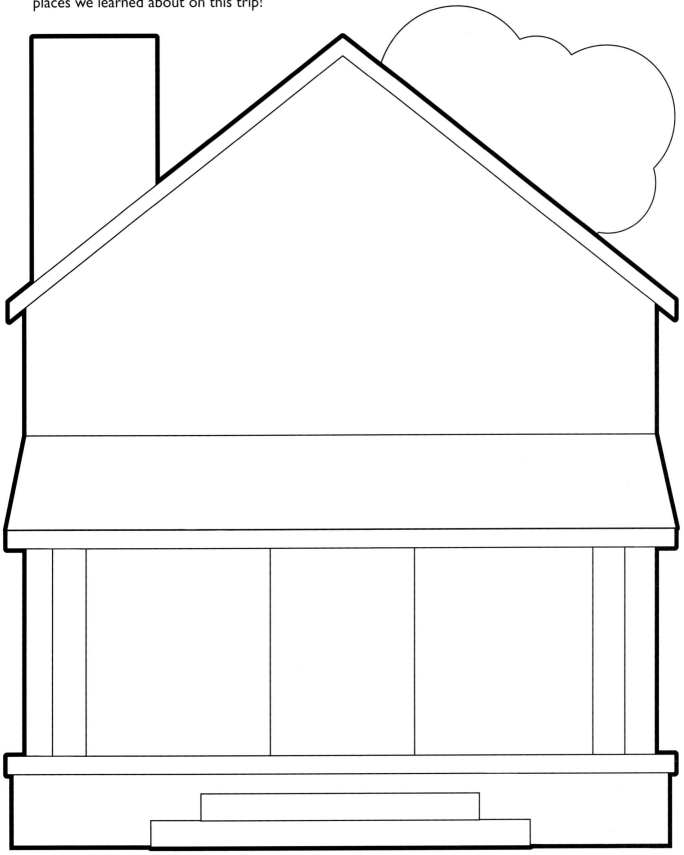

The Transportation Station

Chugga-chugga-chugga…Vroom! Vroom! Whether they have 18 wheels or four, propellers, a stick shift, or no gears at all, youngsters just love things that move! Fasten your seat belt, 'cause you're in for a trip with some unexpected turns!

ADMIT ONE

Getting Ready to Go!

Next stop, the Transportation Station! But wait! You'll need to pack a few things for this trip to the place where wheels and engines reign! Check the lists on page 27; then gather the materials you'll need for the centers you choose. Here are a few more tips to get you ready to roll.

ADMIT ONE

On the Road

Pave the way for fun in your room by creating a roadway all around it! Cut sheets of black construction paper into straight and curved sections; then add yellow paint center lines. Place the road pieces strategically on the floor to follow traffic patterns. Then use clear Con-Tact® covering to adhere the road to the floor. Add some yield and stop signs to control the traffic flow, if necessary.

Transportation Trimmings

Race to your nearest gas station or car dealership and ask for some black-and-white checkered flags or streamers. They'll be happy to share them with future customers! You might also ask for some posters of vehicles to post in your room.

Fuel Up!

Your little drivers won't get far without fuel, so begin looking for some large boxes to transform into gas pumps for the center described in "Fill 'er Up!" on page 33. While you're at it, ask parents or school volunteers to help you round up a tire pump and a couple of squeegees to complete this center.

Transportation Take-Alongs

Choose from the center ideas on pages 28–33. Here's a handy list of the supplies you'll need to prepare each one.

Art Area

Chart Your Course: maps, markers

Map Out a Collage: yellow masking tape or Con-Tact® paper, black construction paper, magazines, scissors, glue sticks

On Your Mark, Get Set…: large piece of black plastic such as a trash bag, tape, yellow tempera paint, dish detergent, toy cars and trucks, construction paper

Round and Round We Go: scissors, paper circles, lazy Susan turntable, bingo markers, tape, washable markers or chalk (optional)

Reading Center

While You're Waiting…: magazine rack; travel magazines, brochures, and posters

Dramatic-Play Center

Take Your Seats, Please: masking tape; marker; fabric strips; self-adhesive Velcro®; large pictures of a bus, a train, and a plane

Just "Plane" Fun!: microwave dinner trays and their boxes, hot glue gun and glue, dark blazers, airline ticket jackets, self-adhesive Velcro®, gallon-size zippered plastic bags, magazines

Science Center

Flashlight Fun: large box; several flashlights and batteries; red, yellow, and green cellophane; rubber bands

Sensory Tables and Tubs

What's Afloat?: food coloring, chunks of thick Styrofoam®, coffee stirring sticks, colored Con-Tact® paper, spray bottles

Up in the Clouds: stuffing from a beanbag chair, liquid dish detergent or extra-strength bubble bath, large plastic serving spoons or rubber spatulas, paper airplanes, swimming goggles

Off to Work We Go: play sand, toy dump trucks and other construction vehicles

Music and Movement

Let the Good Times Roll!: recorded music

Writing Center

Around the World in a…: bulletin board paper, markers, crayons

In My Magic Car: paper, crayons, magazines, scissors, glue sticks

Block Area

Fill 'er Up!: large boxes, paint and paintbrushes, permanent marker, lengths of thick rope, hose nozzles, masking tape, air pump, squeegees

Fine-motor skills
Color and shape discrimination
Creative thinking

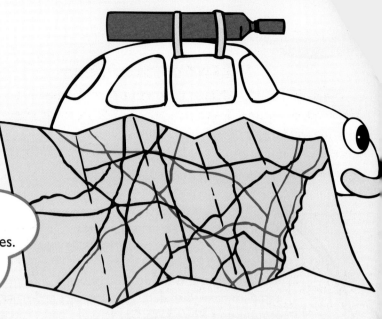

Chart Your Course

Children love to draw on maps! Collect a bunch from motor clubs, gas stations, parents, and magazines. Set them out with markers and have youngsters follow the roads to wherever they lead!

Map Out a Collage

Cut or tear strips of yellow masking tape or yellow Con-Tact® paper. Invite children to make their own maps by randomly sticking the tape or adhesive paper onto black construction paper. Have them add some cars, trucks, or trains cut from magazines to complete their collages.

On Your Mark, Get Set...

And *go* right to this station for some "wheel-y" fun painting! Tape a large piece of black plastic to a tabletop. Pour on a small puddle of yellow tempera paint (mixed with some liquid detergent to keep it from drying out too fast). Add a few toy cars and trucks and let the race begin—the race to make a masterpiece, that is! A young artist can keep part of his design by pressing a piece of paper over the painted tracks to make a monoprint.

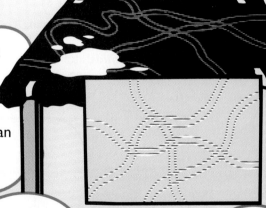

Round and Round We Go

It'll take two drivers working together to operate the "wheel" for this center. Cut a class supply of paper circles; then stick one at a time to a lazy Susan. Have one child in a pair paint the circle with a bingo marker while the other spins the tray. Then tape on a new circle and have the children switch places. As a variation, use washable markers or chalk to decorate the circles.

While You're Waiting...

What do you do while you're waiting for the plane, train, or bus? You read, of course! Transform your reading center into a waiting area in *your* favorite transportation station. Place some chairs in rows and add a magazine rack filled with magazines about travel and tourism. Your local travel agency will probably be happy to supply some magazines, brochures, and posters to complete the look. (Recycle them for your art area later.)

Reading Center

Vocabulary development
Attention span
Collaborative play
Receptive and expressive language skills

Transportation Tales

Travel to your favorite library or bookstore and pick up these books about ways to go. After storytime, transport them to your reading center for little ones to enjoy on a second visit!

Truck Talk
By Bobbi Katz
Published by Cartwheel Books

The Little Engine That Could
By Watty Piper
Published by Grosset & Dunlap

Wheels on the Bus
A Raffi Songs to Read Book
By Raffi
Published by Crown Publishers, Inc.

Flying
By Donald Crews
Published by Mulberry Books

Richard Scarry's Longest Book Ever
By Richard Scarry
Published by Little Simon

Dramatic-Play Center

Collaborative play
Language development
Word/picture association
Socialization

Take Your Seats, Please

How would your little ones like to travel today? By train? Plane? Or bus? Set up some chairs in rows to create aisle and window seating. Label the seats with letters and/or numbers for literacy-building fun. Equip each seat with a safety belt fashioned from a strip of fabric and some self-adhesive Velcro®. Then find some big pictures of a bus, a train, and a plane. Laminate them and put them in the center. When a group of youngsters is ready to pretend, have them select a vehicle picture and hang it on the wall or prop it up at the entrance to the center. Hey, it's a train today—let's chug on over!

Fasten
Seat
Belts

Just "Plane" Fun!

Setting up an airplane in your dramatic-play center? Add these props to enhance children's play. Collect a bunch of microwave dinner trays and the boxes they came in. Hot-glue the box tops to the trays to make portable airplane food! Your young flight attendants can sort, stack, and serve these over and over! Rustle up a couple of dark blazers for flight attendant uniforms and ask a local airline for some ticket jackets. Use strips of self-adhesive Velcro® to attach gallon-size zippered plastic bags to the backs of the airplane seats (chairs set in rows); then place a magazine in each one. Watch the dramatic play take off!

Analytical and creative thinking
Language development
Exploration of cause and effect
Collaborative play

What's Afloat?

Fill a shallow pool or sensory table with tinted water. Make some "boats" by cutting chunks of thick Styrofoam® from packing materials. Add waterproof sails by wrapping colored Con-Tact® paper around plastic coffee stirring sticks. Invite youngsters at this center to maneuver the boats by squirting water from spray bottles. Teach children how to unscrew and refill the bottles for a self-managed center and hours of fun!

Up in the Clouds

What can you do with those wonderful beanbag chairs after they get holes in them? Make clouds! Empty a chair's stuffing into a sensory table or baby pool; then fill it halfway with water and add two cups of liquid dish detergent or extra-strength bubble bath. Collect some large plastic serving spoons or rubber spatulas. Your cloud makers can stir, swirl, and scoop to their hearts' delight! Hang a few paper airplanes overhead and be sure to have some pilot's goggles (swimming goggles) nearby. If the clouds settle overnight, rejuvenate them with a little more water and they'll soon be lighter than air again!

Off to Work We Go

Although it's a staple of any young child's outdoor play, sand takes on new excitement when it comes indoors in a shallow pool with a bit of water added! Bring on the toy dump trucks, bulldozers, and cement mixers. Ready? Let's transport some sand!

31

Writing Center

Creative language and thought processing
Word association
Writing skills
Socialization

We went in a wagon.
— Kyle

Then we went on a train.
— Sié

Then we went on a camel.
— Jose

Around the World in a...

How would *you* like to travel around the world? Invite each of your little ones to choose a mode of transportation—maybe a train or a boat or a hot-air balloon or even an elephant ride! Incorporate his choice into an adventurous tale about a class trip around the globe, arriving back at school just in time for car pool, of course! Write the story on a length of bulletin board paper and have youngsters illustrate their travels.

In My Magic Car

Ask youngsters to imagine they each have a magic car designed to take them *anywhere* they'd like to go! Where would it be? Disney World®? Grandma's house? The jungle? Ask them to write individual stories about their trip. Who would go along? What supplies would they bring? Have students illustrate their stories with drawings or magazine pictures.

My magic car took me to the candy store.

Music and Movement

Auditory skills
Gross-motor skills
Rhythm
Socialization

Let the Good Times Roll!

Crank up some music and invite youngsters to pretend to drive cars to the beat, whether it's fast, slow, or in-between. Stop the music and have them put on the brakes. Then have all the drivers switch directions and drive again when the music starts. Have student volunteers take turns calling out different vehicles to imitate, such as a fire truck, a dump truck, a train, a motorcycle, or a convertible.

Socialization
Language development
Motor skills

Fill 'er Up!

Turn your block area into a gas station! Bring out the boxes you collected (see "Fuel Up!" on page 26). Invite your students to help paint and label them to resemble gas pumps. Create hoses from lengths of thick rope with hose nozzles taped to one end. Add an air pump and some squeegees for getting windows sparkling clean! By the way, this gas station can accommodate all kinds of vehicles—even trains and planes!

Science Center

Observation skills
Color and shape discrimination
Exploration of cause and effect

Flashlight Fun

How do cars and trucks "see" at night? With lights, of course! Place a large box in your science area, big enough for children to crawl inside of or at least poke their heads into. Gather several flashlights in various sizes and shapes. Leave some plain and transform others by attaching pieces of red, yellow, or green cellophane over the lights with rubber bands. Invite youngsters to explore with the flashlights inside the dark box. Better ask parents to send in extra batteries, 'cause you'll *definitely* need them!

Tips for an Extended Stay

When your centers are ready to fly, try these ideas for a
group activity, some outdoor fun, and a family activity.

All Together Now

Encourage your class to create its own original flying,
floating, or freewheeling form of transportation! Start
with a big box or several smaller ones that children
can sit inside of. Supply paint, glue, aluminum foil,
juice can lids, small paper plates, string, and any
other spare craft materials. In no time at all, you'll
have a marvelous machine!

Out 'n' About

If your youngsters liked painting with wheels as described
in "On Your Mark, Get Set…" on page 28, then they'll *love*
this giant-sized art experience! Lay out an old tarp on the
sidewalk or in the parking area. Tuck the end of a roll of
bulletin board paper under one side of the tarp, and unroll a
long length. Pour some paint mixed with liquid dish detergent onto the tarp. Invite a child to drive a toy through the
paint and down the paper runway to create tracks! Add
some more tracks until the paper looks "just right"; then
replace it with a new piece and keep rolling—and painting!
When you're done, turn the play area into a car wash and
have the drivers hose down the vehicles.

Family Focus

Ask parents to join you as youngsters explore one or more of the many ways we get
around. Visit an airport or a train station, or hop on the city bus! Or you could also ask a
limousine service to visit your school or center and take youngsters and parents on a ride
around the block. Some of your parents might even work in jobs that use interesting modes
of transportation. Ask them to bring their work vehicles to school for show-and-tell!

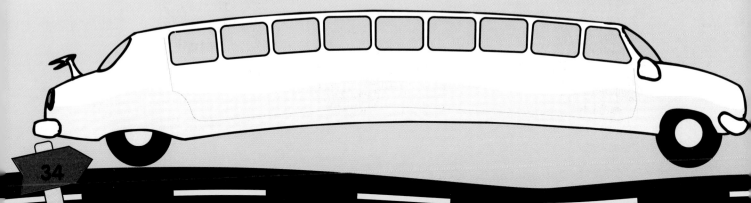

Highlights of Our Trip
The Transportation Station

Chugga-chugga-beep-beep! Hop on board and see what we did when we visited the Transportation Station—right in our very own room!

In a Cozy Kitchen

Slip on an apron and venture into the arena of creative culinary delight! With a heaping cup of imagination and a pinch of preparation, you'll find this trip to the kitchen a truly appetizing adventure!

Getting Ready to Go!

The recipe for success in this kitchen is easy! Just check out the lists on page 37 and gather what you'll need according to the centers you choose to set up. Below are some more helpful hints for making the most of your prep time.

May We Borrow a Cup of Sugar?

Ask parents to donate some of the foodstuffs you'll need for this unit, such as flour, yeast, extracts, bread, pasta, or rice.

And May We Keep the Cup?

And while you're at it, ask for some of the kitchen gear you'll need. Placemats, napkins, pot holders, kitchen towels, and even an old set of kitchen curtains will dress up your dramatic-play area for "At the Dinner Table" on page 40. You'll also need all kinds of kitchen gadgets for several of the centers in this unit, so ask parents to raid their kitchen drawers and send in their castoffs.

What About a *Restaurant* Kitchen?

Not all kitchens are at home, of course! Lend a professional flair to your culinary explorations by asking a local restaurant to donate signature hats, aprons, napkins, food containers, or menus to use as props for children's play.

The Key Ingredients

Choose from the center ideas on pages 38–43. Here's a handy list of the supplies you'll need to prepare each one.

Art Area

Dinner, Anyone?: paper plates, glue sticks, food magazines, scissors

Makes "Scents": small jars; food coloring; extracts; construction paper, paper plates, or tagboard; paintbrushes

"Krazy" Kitchen Art: kitchen gadgets, tempera paint, disposable pie pans, construction paper, cookie sheets, newspaper, smocks

Rolling in the Dough: white bread, tinted glue, spray varnish (optional)

Reading Center

Read With the Chef: chef's apron and toque; cookbooks, magazines, and stories showing food from various cultures

Dramatic-Play Center

Gotta Make the Doughnuts: hats, bags or boxes, and waxed paper sheets from a local bakery or doughnut shop; sponge or foam doughnuts; cookie sheets; oven mitts; empty boxes of powdered sugar; empty bottles of sprinkles; frying pans; spatulas

Mmm…Do I Smell Bread Baking?: uncolored homemade play dough, airtight container, aprons, dull knives, mini loaf pans, wooden cutting board

At the Dinner Table: tablecloth or placemats, cloth napkins, salt and pepper shakers, vase of silk flowers, family photos, cookbooks and/or food magazines

Science Center

Mix 'n' Match-a-roni: pasta in various colors, shapes, and sizes; muffin tin or plastic bowls; hot glue gun and glue

Yes, It's Yeast!: active yeast, sugar, warm water, bowl, magnifying glasses

Writing Center

A Cake for a King: chart paper, markers

Spaghetti Stories: copy paper, stapler, crayons, hole punchers, white yarn

Block Area

Let's Have a Cookout!: toaster oven racks, spatula, oven mitts, platters, paper plates, play food, potatoes wrapped in foil (optional)

Sensory Tables and Tubs

Fun With Flour: flour, sifters, mixing spoons, measuring cups, bowls, smocks, throw rugs

Is It Soup Yet?: Styrofoam® packing peanuts, yellow food coloring, ladles, soup pot, dissolvable packing peanuts (optional)

Oodles of Wet 'n' Wiggly Noodles: cooked pasta, spoons, pasta forks, colanders, serving bowls, construction paper

Rice Is Nice!: rice, measuring cups, slotted spoons, chopsticks, wok

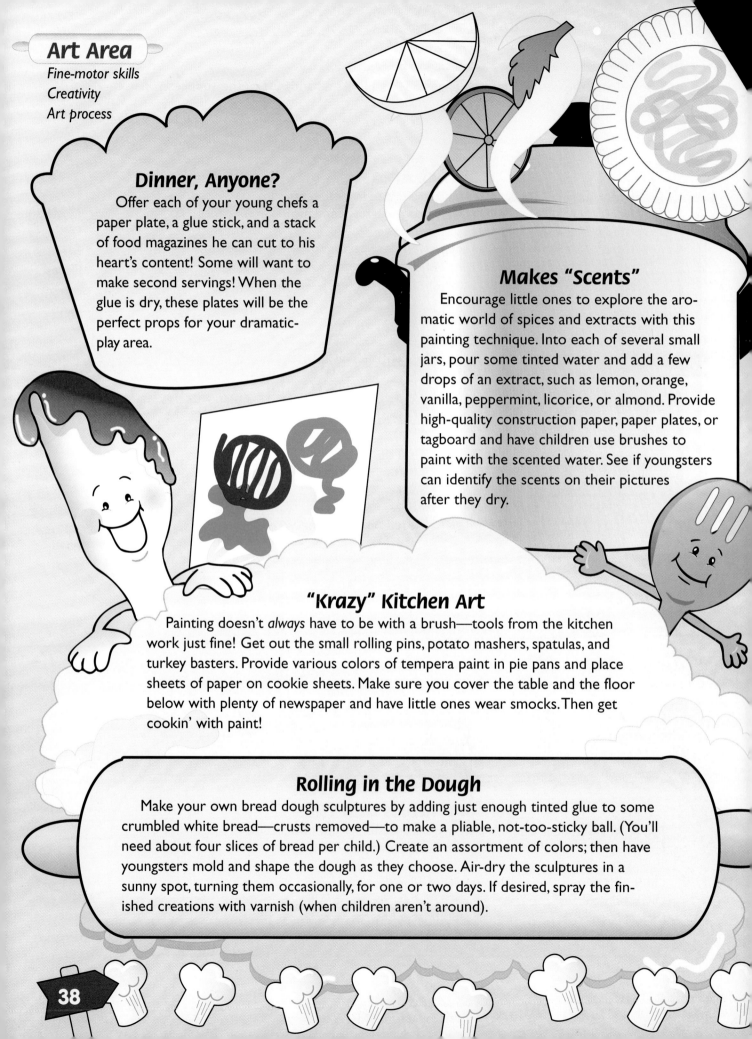

Dinner, Anyone?

Offer each of your young chefs a paper plate, a glue stick, and a stack of food magazines he can cut to his heart's content! Some will want to make second servings! When the glue is dry, these plates will be the perfect props for your dramatic-play area.

Makes "Scents"

Encourage little ones to explore the aromatic world of spices and extracts with this painting technique. Into each of several small jars, pour some tinted water and add a few drops of an extract, such as lemon, orange, vanilla, peppermint, licorice, or almond. Provide high-quality construction paper, paper plates, or tagboard and have children use brushes to paint with the scented water. See if youngsters can identify the scents on their pictures after they dry.

"Krazy" Kitchen Art

Painting doesn't *always* have to be with a brush—tools from the kitchen work just fine! Get out the small rolling pins, potato mashers, spatulas, and turkey basters. Provide various colors of tempera paint in pie pans and place sheets of paper on cookie sheets. Make sure you cover the table and the floor below with plenty of newspaper and have little ones wear smocks. Then get cookin' with paint!

Rolling in the Dough

Make your own bread dough sculptures by adding just enough tinted glue to some crumbled white bread—crusts removed—to make a pliable, not-too-sticky ball. (You'll need about four slices of bread per child.) Create an assortment of colors; then have youngsters mold and shape the dough as they choose. Air-dry the sculptures in a sunny spot, turning them occasionally, for one or two days. If desired, spray the finished creations with varnish (when children aren't around).

Read With the Chef

Wear an apron and a chef's toque (donated by a local restaurant) to storytime. Talk about different types of restaurants and the food they serve. This unit is a great opportunity to talk about similarities and differences in various cultures, and some of the books below will help you get started. When storytime is over, place the apron and hat in your reading center, along with a variety of cookbooks, magazines, and stories that show foods from many different cultures.

Books That Really Cook!

Little ones will eat these food-related stories right up!

Bread Bread Bread
By Ann Morris
Mulberry Books

More Spaghetti, I Say!
By Rita Golden Gelman
Cartwheel Books

Strega Nona
By Tomie dePaola
Aladdin Paperbacks

Lunch
By Denise Fleming
Henry Holt and Company

Peanut Butter and Jelly: A Play Rhyme
Illustrated by Nadine Bernard Westcott
E. P. Dutton

Pancakes for Breakfast
By Tomie dePaola
Harcourt Brace & Company

Dramatic-Play Center

Tactile exploration
Language development
Creative thinking
Socialization

Mmm…Do I Smell Bread Baking?

Supply your young cooks with some bread dough they can knead, shape, and bake for weeks! Have youngsters assist you in preparing a batch of your favorite homemade play dough *without* adding coloring. Store this in an airtight container in your dramatic-play area. Also provide aprons, knives, mini loaf pans, and a wooden cutting board. This is sure to be the coziest spot in your classroom!

Gotta Make the Doughnuts

Transform your dramatic-play area into a doughnut shop! Visit your local bakery or doughnut shop and collect some disposable hats, doughnut bags or boxes, and a supply of waxed paper sheets (you know, doughnut-picker-uppers!). To make doughnuts your little bakers can cook time and again, cut doughnut shapes from large sponges or foam sold by the foot at a fabric store. Also supply cookie sheets, oven mitts, empty boxes of powdered sugar, empty bottles of sprinkles, big frying pans, and spatulas. What fun!

At the Dinner Table

Sure, you have a kitchen in the dramatic-play center almost all the time, but this time, really make it look like home! Use a tablecloth or placemats, and set out cloth napkins, salt and pepper shakers, and a vase of silk flowers. Hang some family photos on a wall and stack some cookbooks or food magazines on a counter. Be sure to serve the home-cooked meals prepared in the art area (see "Dinner, Anyone?" on page 38).

Fun With Flour

Put some flour—okay, *a lot* of flour—in a sensory table or tub, along with real flour sifters, big mixing spoons, measuring cups, and bowls. Have youngsters wear smocks and cover the area below the table with some throw rugs that can be shaken out periodically. When you're through with this center, bag up the flour and save it for making nonedible play dough!

Oodles of Wet 'n' Wiggly Noodles

For a messy but delightful sensory experience, fill a tub with cooked noodles! Provide big spoons, pasta forks, colanders, and serving bowls. Instruct children that this pasta is for "cooking," not eating. Then let them explore the properties of pasta! After some time to play, invite each child to stick some wet pasta onto construction paper in the design of her choice. The starchy noodles will stick without glue—it's true!

Is It Soup Yet?

Dumplings come in all shapes...even those that look remarkably like packing peanuts! Float several handfuls of recycled Styrofoam® peanuts in yellow-tinted water—the broth, of course! Toss in some soup ladles and a big soup pot for stirring and serving. For a *really* original soup of the day, throw in some dissolvable packing peanuts and stir up a new concoction!

Rice Is Nice!

Around the world, you'll find rice in almost every culture's kitchen. Fill a tub or sensory table with a few big bags of rice and toss in measuring cups, slotted spoons, chopsticks, and a wok. Your master chefs will whip up some rice dishes in no time! When you're done with this center, dye the rice and use it in your art area as a substitute for glitter.

Creative thinking
Word association
Writing skills
Socialization

A King's Cake

18 cups flour
20 cups sugar
2 eggs

6 candy bars
a little water
a bottle of milk

Stir everything up with a spoon.
Put it in a pan and cook it in the oven
at 1,000 degrees for 2 hours.
Put on a lot of frosting
and candles.

A Cake for a King

Let's all bake a delectable cake, one that's fit for a king! What in the world would we put in it? Ask your youngsters and they'll come up with a *most* interesting recipe! Write it on a large sheet of chart paper as they dictate it. Ask them to add an illustration of the finished cake. Hang this up for all to see—and to copy, of course, if they'd like to make it in their own kitchens!

Spaghetti Stories

After reading the pasta-themed stories from the list on page 39, ask your young writers to make up their own stories about the possibilities of pasta. Give each child a blank book (a few sheets of copy paper stapled together) in which to write or draw his story. Add a fun touch by providing hole punchers and long strands of white yarn. Have youngsters punch holes in their finished pages and weave the yarn in and out as they choose. Watch out—spaghetti on the loose!

Mix 'n' Match-a-roni

Concoct a matching game with a variety of colors, sizes, and shapes of pasta. Hot-glue a different type or color of pasta to the bottom of each cup in a muffin tin (or to the bottom of individual plastic bowls). Then dump the remaining pasta in your collection into a big bowl for children to sort.

Yes, It's Yeast!

Add active yeast and a bit of sugar to warm water according to package directions. Encourage little ones to observe the changes that take place over time and to describe what they see happening. Have some magnifying glasses at this center for the extra curious investigators.

Let's Have a Cookout!

Sometimes it's fun to take the kitchen outdoors—or at least *pretend* to! The block area is the perfect site for grilling. Have youngsters construct an open square for the grill's brick base. Provide toaster oven racks to serve as the grill racks. And don't forget a spatula, oven mitts, platters, and paper plates. Real potatoes can be wrapped in foil and grilled for weeks, but play food is just as fun, too!

Tips for an Extended Stay

When you have your classroom centers cookin', plan to add these ideas for a group project, an outdoor jaunt, and a family activity.

All Together Now

It's time to bake some *real* bread! Let your busy bakers assist in making a batch of bread, whether it's a traditional loaf or something like biscuits, corn bread, flatbread, or pizza dough. This is best done in small groups and several batches so that every child gets to help *a lot*. Start early and when it's done, you can all enjoy it together before the day is through!

Out 'n' About

Take the cooking outdoors when you plan a make-your-own sandwich picnic! Pack a basket with the fixings for peanut butter and jelly sandwiches (or something else just as easy). Go out to your play area, spread a blanket, and set out the ingredients. Then watch your little chefs go to work preparing their own lunches. Mmm…it tastes so good when you make it yourself!

Terrific Tossed Salad

3 carrots

2 tomatoes, sliced

1 head of lettuce torn

1 chopped apple

2 sliced cucumbers

Family Focus

Invite a few parents to share some of their own tricks in the kitchen. Have each visitor prepare a simple dish as your little ones watch or perhaps give a little help. Write the recipe on chart paper beforehand, adding simple drawings of the ingredients to help prereaders follow along. Take some photos and attach a developed picture to a thank-you note from the class.

Highlights of Our Trip
In a Cozy Kitchen

With just a pinch of *this* and a cup of *that,* we created all kinds of culinary concoctions! Want to know our original recipes for fun? Read below!

©2000 The Education Center, Inc. • *More Classroom Adventures* • TEC897

Land of the Giants

Fee-fi-fo-fum—we're looking for giants! Whoa! Here they come! Imaginations will soar as children begin comparing the GIGANTIC to the teeny-tiny. Your young mathematicians will be learning about size concepts while they have fun, fun, fun on this adventure!

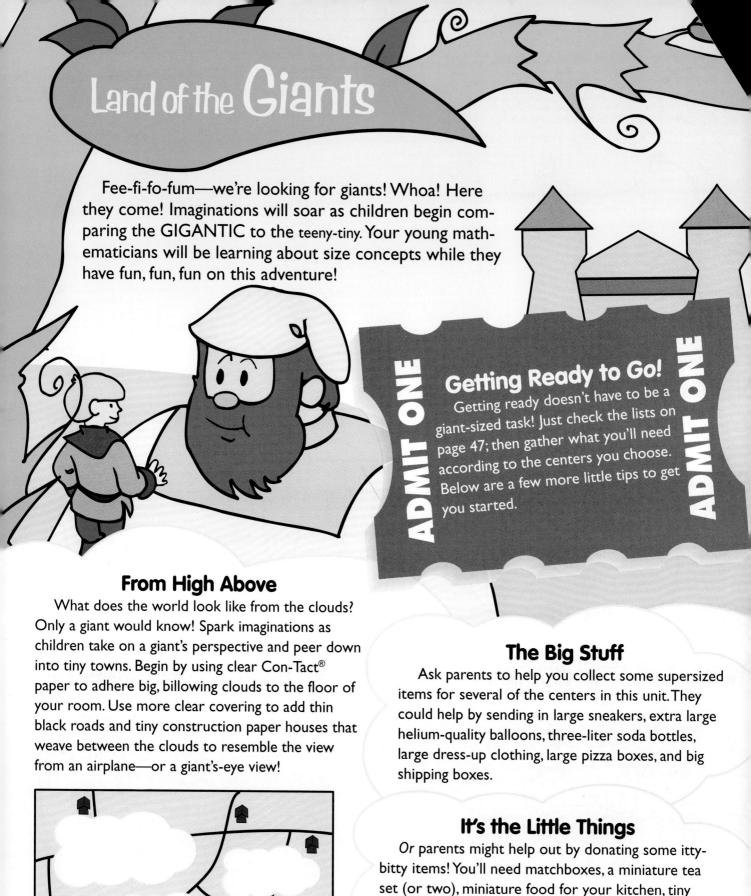

Getting Ready to Go!

Getting ready doesn't have to be a giant-sized task! Just check the lists on page 47; then gather what you'll need according to the centers you choose. Below are a few more little tips to get you started.

ADMIT ONE

ADMIT ONE

From High Above

What does the world look like from the clouds? Only a giant would know! Spark imaginations as children take on a giant's perspective and peer down into tiny towns. Begin by using clear Con-Tact® paper to adhere big, billowing clouds to the floor of your room. Use more clear covering to add thin black roads and tiny construction paper houses that weave between the clouds to resemble the view from an airplane—or a giant's-eye view!

The Big Stuff

Ask parents to help you collect some supersized items for several of the centers in this unit. They could help by sending in large sneakers, extra large helium-quality balloons, three-liter soda bottles, large dress-up clothing, large pizza boxes, and big shipping boxes.

It's the Little Things

Or parents might help out by donating some itty-bitty items! You'll need matchboxes, a miniature tea set (or two), miniature food for your kitchen, tiny paper plates, and tiny pencils like those used in golf.

Supplies of Every Size

Choose from the center ideas on pages 48–53. Here's a handy list of the supplies you'll need to prepare each one.

Art Area

Now That's a Big Foot!: large sneakers or clown shoes, tray of tempera paint, butcher paper or newspaper

A Teeny-Tiny Bed: matchboxes, glue sticks, fabric squares, cotton batting

Great Big Body Pictures: lamp or overhead projector, bulletin board paper, markers, crayons, chalk (optional)

Eek! It's Shrinking!: Aleene's® Shrink-It™ plastic sheets, scissors, permanent markers, oven

Reading Center

Books of Every Size: big books, tiny books, poster board, scissors, hole puncher, yarn, thread, markers

Dramatic-Play Center

Teatime: large shoes, hats, scarves, and gloves; miniature tea set(s); small paper plates; napkins; scissors; tiny toy food

And for the Big Appetite…: large pizza boxes, buckets from fast-food chicken restaurants, take-out containers from Chinese restaurants, boxes from children's fast-food meals, cardboard pizza rounds, markers, construction paper, glue

Science Center

Now It's Big…Now It's Not!: various sizes of clear plastic soda bottles; fillers in various sizes (tiny beads, wooden beads, marbles, small Nerf® balls, etc.); hot glue gun and glue

Music and Movement

At the Giants' Ball: large shoes, recordings of classical music

Writing Center

Here's the Rest of the Story…: chart paper, thick markers

Teeny-Tiny Tales, Too!: two- or three-inch square pieces of copy paper and construction paper, stapler, golf pencils or skinny markers

Sensory Tables and Tubs

Beads in a Bottle (or Cup): small plastic beads, tweezers, clear 16-ounce soda bottles or small drinking cups

Ping-Pong® Balls in a Pool: Ping-Pong® balls (colored or decorated with markers), plastic tongs, big plastic pitchers

Ooey Gooey and Gargantuan!: one gallon Elmer's® school glue, three quarts liquid starch, food coloring

Beluga "Balloon-as": extra large helium-quality balloons; a baby pool; liquid dish detergent; sequins, foil confetti, or colorful plastic beads (optional)

Block Area

Itty-Bitty Autos: small wooden blocks, Con-Tact® paper, scissors

Supersize It: large shipping boxes, masking tape, liquid tempera paint, glue, paintbrushes

Art Area

Size and shape discrimination
Fine-motor skills
Language development
Socialization

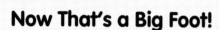

A Teeny-Tiny Bed

Each of your little artists will love making a teeny-tiny bed for a teeny-tiny mouse. Give each child a matchbox and help her create a cozy bed by using a glue stick to cover the box with a tiny square of fabric. Have her tuck a bit of cotton batting into the box for a warm, fuzzy blanket. Then wait for the mouse to come!

Now That's a Big Foot!

Youngsters can make giant footprints when they're wearing the giant's shoes! Get an old pair of sneakers from a very tall dad or purchase a pair of clown shoes at a party store. Have a child step into the shoes, then into a shallow tray of tempera paint, and finally onto a long length of butcher paper or a trail of newspaper. Wow! Look at the size of those prints! Be sure to have *plenty* of paper because everyone will want to try!

Great Big Body Pictures

Invite children to make ENORMOUS shadows when you shine a lamp or overhead projector onto a blank wall or a film screen. Post a length of bulletin board paper on the wall and trace around part of each child's shadow. Invite little ones to color their shadows and hang them up for classmates to see. Can they guess which shadow belongs to which child?

As a variation, you can try capturing shadows outdoors on a sunny sidewalk. BIG fun!

Eek! It's Shrinking!

For a fun and scientific art experience, purchase a package of Aleene's® Shrink-It™ at your local craft store. Cut the plastic sheets into large, simple shapes and then invite each artist to use permanent markers to decorate one as she desires. Bake the shapes as directed on the package. Once they've cooled, have youngsters see if they can find their shrunken creations.

Books of Every Size

This is the time to highlight all the fun sizes books come in, from jumbo big books to those little bitty gift books. Have some of each in your reading center. For fun, cut giant bookmarks from poster board and add a long, thick tassel of yarn to one end of each one. Cut teeny bookmarks from the poster board scraps and add a tiny thread tassel to each one. Embellish these with appropriate phrases and put them in the center.

Reading is ENORMOUS FUN!

Read a little—it's FUN!

Size Up These Books

Storytime is bound to be big fun when you share one of these delightful stories! After reading them aloud, place them in your reading center for your young readers to enjoy again.

David's Father
By Robert Munsch
Firefly Books Ltd.

The Enormous Potato
By Aubrey Davis
Kids Can Press

Jack and the Beanstalk
By Paul Galdone
Houghton Mifflin Company

The Teeny-Tiny Woman
By Harriet Ziefert
Puffin Books

The NBA Book of Big and Little
By James Preller
Scholastic Inc.

Dramatic-Play Center

Collaborative play
Size discrimination
Socialization

Teatime

Ever been to a giant's tea party? Ever *been the giant* at a tea party? Your little ones can experience gigantic fun at this one! Have extra large shoes, scarves, hats, and gloves (or other appropriate dress for giants) available for children. Then bring out a miniature tea set (or two if you have lots of guests!), as well as the smallest plates you can find and napkins cut down to a tiny size. Replace the play food in the kitchen cupboards with tiny toy food. Welcome, giants! Won't you have a sip of tea?

And for the Big Appetite...

Of course, a real giant wouldn't be satisfied with the tea party goodies us regular folks might like. So bring on a giant-sized supper—you know, several large pizzas, some buckets of chicken, a few containers of Chinese takeout, and maybe a few fast-food kids' meals, too! Have your little cooks prepare the pizzas by decorating cardboard pizza rounds donated by a local pizza parlor. Ask other eating establishments or parents to donate the other food containers. Then watch as your youngsters role-play hungry giants—and show off their knowledge of environmental print as well!

Pizza

Fried Chicken

Sensory Tables and Tubs
Fine-motor skills
Sorting
Tactile exploration
Weight discrimination
Socialization

Beads in a Bottle (or Cup)

Have youngsters try their hands at some teeny-tiny fine-motor coordination. Fill a sensory tub with small plastic or pony beads. Supply tweezers and some clear plastic 16-ounce soda bottles or very small drinking cups. Ask little ones to use the tweezers to pick up the beads and sort them by color into the containers. For a real challenge, float the beads in water!

Note: Small beads can be a choking hazard for very young children. Provide adequate supervision.

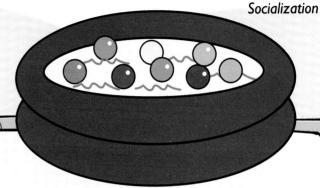

Ooey Gooey and Gargantuan!

For an extra special treat for the entire school, make a giant amount of putty. Add one gallon of Elmer's® school glue (absolutely no substitutes will do) to three quarts of liquid starch. Tint it pink and call it the giant's bubble gum. Tint it yellow and it's a huge plate of scrambled eggs! The more you knead it, the firmer it will get. If it's too sticky, add more starch. This putty will last for weeks if you occasionally add more starch and refrigerate it on the weekends. It's too big *not* to share, so pass it from class to class. Teeny-tiny toddlers to great big afterschoolers will love it!

Ping-Pong® Balls in a Pool

For a fun comparison to the activity in "Beads in a Bottle (or Cup)", fill a baby pool with Ping-Pong® balls. Supply plastic tongs (the *giant's* tweezers!) and big plastic pitchers for containers. Add a splash of water to this center, too, if you like. To add the sorting skill to this center, purchase colored Ping-Pong balls at a sporting goods store or use permanent markers to draw colorful designs on white ones.

Beluga "Balloon-as"!

Be adventurous and try this whale of a water-balloon activity! Buy a few extra large helium-quality balloons (the kind that party stores use to float baskets). Fill them with water and add them to a baby pool. Add enough water and liquid dish detergent to the pool to make the balloons slippery. They'll be too heavy (and too slippery) for little ones to pick up, but boy, will they have fun trying! For added fun, try to find transparent balloons and slip in some sequins, foil confetti, or colorful plastic beads before you fill them with water.

Science Center

Size and weight discrimination
Observation skills

Now It's Big...Now It's Not!

Clear plastic soda bottles make for a fun study of light refraction. Start with a 16-ounce bottle and drop in some tiny beads before filling it with water and hot-gluing the cap in place. Prepare more bottles in varying sizes, ending with a three-liter bottle with large marbles or small Nerf® balls inside. Have youngsters examine the bottles and see how objects appear magnified.

Block Area

Collaborative play
Motor skills
Size and shape discrimination

Supersize It

For supersized block building, collect a bunch of large shipping boxes and tape them shut. Paint them with a mixture of two parts liquid tempera paint to one part white school glue for durable, smudge-free constructions. Don't be afraid to use *really* big boxes—little builders love a giant-sized task!

Itty-Bitty Autos

Here's a safe alternative to tiny toy cars—and these are custom-made! Pick out your smallest wooden blocks; then cut wheels and headlights from Con-Tact® paper to fit them. Help little ones stick on the details; then put the revved-up blocks in your block area. Watch how big the roads and buildings become around children as they build!

Highlights of Our Trip
Land of the Giants

We've just come back from a trip of gigantic proportions! And we have a *really* tall tale to tell! Read on…

At the Construction Site

From drawing the blueprints to hanging the curtains, building a house—or any other structure—is a big job! Invite your students to come see how it's done and have some fun!

SLOW

Getting Ready to Go!

You'll need some materials and tools to construct this unit, so check out the lists on page 57. Then gather what you need according to the centers you choose. Use the ideas below to make your construction site more authentic.

Under Construction

Create construction zones in your classroom by marking off your centers with plastic cones from your playground, boundary tape, or sections of plastic lattice fencing (available at home improvement stores).

Building Props

Add a pair of sawhorses to your block area or outdoor play yard. Check with parents or ask a local hardware store or home improvement store to donate these. You might also ask for help collecting some other building props, such as wood scraps, roofing paper, plastic tubing, PVC pipes, pulleys, and the materials to make "The Paint and Paper Store" (page 63) come to life.

Dressing the Part

At the construction site, it's so important to be safe. See if you can round up a class supply of children's costume hard hats. Youngsters will love wearing these throughout the unit!

Construction Collectibles

Choose from the center ideas on pages 58–63. Here's a handy list of the supplies you'll need to prepare each one.

READY MIX CONCRETE

Art Area

Real Blueprints: blueprints, rulers, markers, pencils

Not-So-Real Blueprints: wooden blocks or Styrofoam® pieces in various shapes, blue tempera paint, shallow trays, white construction paper

Make a Model: pieces of sturdy cardboard, wood scraps, cardboard shapes, mat board shapes, sandpaper, craft sticks, aluminum foil, "glue" tinted brown or gray (see page 4)

Easel Explorations: black roofing paper; oil pastels, sugar chalk, or builder's chalk

Dramatic-Play Center

The Paint and Paper Store: painters' caps, aprons, paint sticks, wallpaper sample books, sample paint chips, paintbrushes, rollers, paint trays, sponges, sand buckets or cylindrical ice-cream cartons, toy cash register, play money

Interior Design by…You!: box of accessories (pillows, curtains, baskets, silk plants, etc.)

Science Center

Pulley Play: pulley, rope or string, bucket, baby pool, play sand

Reading Center

Building Literacy: hard hat, work boots, toolbox, construction stories

Music and Movement

Build to the Music: children's costume hard hats, toy hammers, paintbrushes, squeegees, disposable pie plates, recorded music

Writing Center

Our Dream Home: newspaper ads for home-improvement stores, scissors, bulletin board paper, glue sticks, markers

My Toolbox: 5½" x 11" sheets of copy paper and 6" x 12" sheets of construction paper, pipe cleaners, stapler or tape, crayons, magazines, scissors, glue

Sensory Tables and Tubs

Funnels Are Fun!: play sand, small pebbles, toy trucks, funnels, string, small shovels

Concrete Concoction: play sand, corn-starch, water, bucket(s), smocks

Pipes and Pebbles: aquarium pebbles, various sizes of plastic tubing and PVC pipe

Pipes and Pebbles and Puddles: aquarium pebbles, various sizes of plastic tubing and PVC pipe, plastic soda bottle funnels, water, food coloring

Block Area

Off to Work We Go…: wheelbarrow or wagon, wooden blocks, toy hammers, tape measure, safety goggles, tool belts, children's costume hard hats, children's work boots, caution signs, boundary tape

Art Area

Color and shape recognition
Cognitive skills
Creative expression
Language development

Not-So-Real Blueprints

Invite little ones to make their own blueprints. Collect wooden blocks or Styrofoam® pieces in a variety of shapes. Set out a shallow tray of blue tempera paint and some large sheets of white construction paper. Invite each little architect to dip the shapes of his choice into paint and then onto the paper to create an original building design.

Real Blueprints

Get a box full of real blueprints from an architecture school or a construction company. Leave them actual size or cut them down to make them a bit more manageable. Add a few rulers and different sizes of markers and pencils; then watch little ones go to work!

Make a Model

For three-dimensional versions of building plans, youngsters can create models. Give each artist a piece of sturdy cardboard for a base. Supply thin wood scraps, cardboard shapes, shapes cut from mat board, sandpaper, craft sticks, aluminum foil, and anything else in your craft closet that seems appropriate! Have youngsters use "plue" (see page 4) tinted brown or gray to cement their models together.

Easel Explorations

Cut some black roofing paper (available at home improvement stores) to fit your easel. Provide oil pastels, sugar chalk (see page 5), or builder's chalk (from a hardware store) for drawing designs. Hang the finished masterpieces around your room.

Building Literacy

Show up for storytime dressed in a hard hat and work boots. Bring along a toolbox filled with construction stories. Then proceed to build up your little ones' imaginations, vocabularies, and language skills! After reading to your students, place the book-filled toolbox in your reading area.

Books About Building

Encourage your curious young builders to seek more information in these books about building everything from houses to skyscrapers.

Construction Zone
By Tana Hoban
Greenwillow Books

Building a House
By Byron Barton
Mulberry Books

Into the Sky
By Ryan Ann Hunter
Holiday House, Inc.

Bam Bam Bam
By Eve Merriam
Henry Holt and Company

Houses and Homes
By Ann Morris
Mulberry Books

Science Center

Analytical thinking
Exploring cause and effect
Simple machines

Pulley Play

Children are fascinated with pulleys—an essential machine for every construction site! Purchase a pulley at your local hardware or home improvement store and set it up in your science area. Tie a lightweight bucket to one end of a sturdy string or rope and then feed the string or rope through the pulley. Tie a loop handle in the opposite end. Place a shallow pool of sand below the bucket so youngsters can fill, pull, and dump...over and over again!

Writing Center

Language development
Fine-motor skills
Sequencing
Writing skills

Our Dream Home

Save the home improvement store ads from the Sunday paper and put them to use as you write a class story about building a dream house. Have each child cut out a picture of an item or a material she'd like to add to the house. Roll out a length of bulletin board paper and invite each child to glue down her picture and write or dictate about it. Before long, you'll have all the parts to make a very *interesting* home!

Special cabinet to lock up my toys

Lots of chairs my size

The house will have a tower.

My Toolbox

Every carpenter has a special toolbox—the real fun begins when you find out what's inside! For each child, staple together a few 5½" x 11" sheets of copy paper between two 6" x 12" sheets of construction paper. Then staple or tape a pipe-cleaner handle to the construction paper cover, so that the book resembles a toolbox. Invite each young author to create his own magical toolbox by either drawing or cutting and pasting pictures on each page. The tools can be as true-to-life or as silly as youngsters wish. Be sure to have them share the contents with classmates!

My Toolbox by Theo

60

Funnels Are Fun!

Sand is always a hit, but this time it's a prime ingredient in concrete! Fill a sensory table or sturdy plastic pool with clean play sand. Add some small pebbles for texture interest. Park a collection of toy trucks in this tub. Then hang some funnels from the ceiling, so that they are suspended just above the sand. Toss in a few small shovels and let your little ones loose!

Pipes and Pebbles

Pour a few bags of aquarium pebbles into a tub. Then supply different sizes of plastic tubing and PVC pipe. Plink, plink, plunk! What wonderful sounds those pebbles make as they travel through the tunnels and tubes!

Concrete Concoction

Create a wet, almost-as-good-as-real-cement concoction of cornstarch, sand, and water. This variation of the infamous "goop" will have your construction workers busier than ants! Start with a bucket of sand, add three or four boxes of cornstarch, and then add water until the consistency seems right for wet cement. Have your little ones wear smocks and be sure to have a clean bucket of water near this station for hand rinsing *before* youngsters make a trip to the classroom sink for a more thorough cleanup.

Pipes and Pebbles and Puddles

Set up a center similar to the one above, but this time add water. A few drops of food coloring will make it all the more interesting! And toss in some homemade funnels, made by carefully cutting the base from plastic soda bottles (any size).

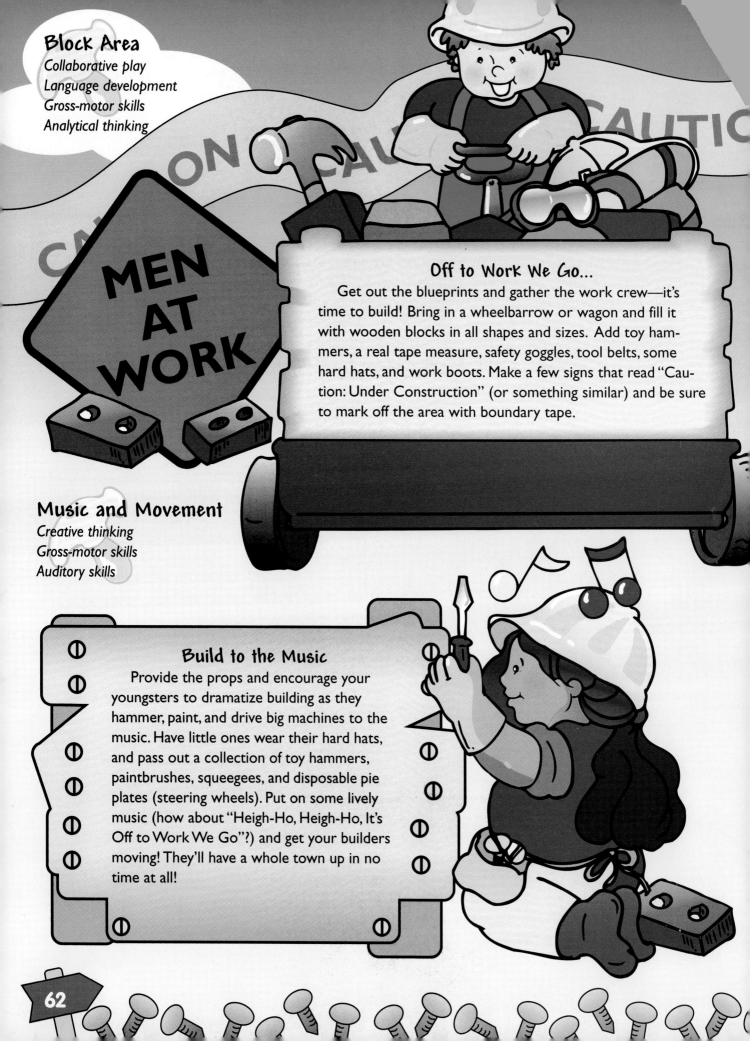

Block Area

Collaborative play
Language development
Gross-motor skills
Analytical thinking

MEN AT WORK

Off to Work We Go...

Get out the blueprints and gather the work crew—it's time to build! Bring in a wheelbarrow or wagon and fill it with wooden blocks in all shapes and sizes. Add toy hammers, a real tape measure, safety goggles, tool belts, some hard hats, and work boots. Make a few signs that read "Caution: Under Construction" (or something similar) and be sure to mark off the area with boundary tape.

Music and Movement

Creative thinking
Gross-motor skills
Auditory skills

Build to the Music

Provide the props and encourage your youngsters to dramatize building as they hammer, paint, and drive big machines to the music. Have little ones wear their hard hats, and pass out a collection of toy hammers, paintbrushes, squeegees, and disposable pie plates (steering wheels). Put on some lively music (how about "Heigh-Ho, Heigh-Ho, It's Off to Work We Go"?) and get your builders moving! They'll have a whole town up in no time at all!

The Paint and Paper Store

Transform your dramatic-play area into a paint and wallpaper shop, so builders and decorators can come by for all those supplies they need. Ask a local store to donate painters' caps, aprons, paint sticks, and old wallpaper books, as well as sample paint chips. Add some brushes, rollers, paint trays, and sponges. Sand buckets or cylindrical ice-cream cartons make fine paint cans! Be sure you have a toy cash register and play money on hand so builders and decorators can buy, buy, buy!

Interior Design by...You!

Once the house is built, it's time to turn it into a *home!* Give your youngsters an opportunity to do their own interior designing by adding a big box of accessories to your housekeeping area. Toss in decorative pillows, old kitchen curtains, a variety of baskets, silk plants, unbreakable picture frames, throw rugs, and any other items you have in the attic or garage that might be perfect for your little designers' decorating plans. Encourage little ones to pick, choose, and place to make the area look *just right*.

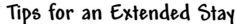

Tips for an Extended Stay

After you've constructed your classroom centers, try these ideas for a group project, outdoor fun, and a parent involvement activity.

All Together Now

Gather your work force to construct a city—the fast way! First, have youngsters make small building shapes or road signs from mat board, craft sticks, Styrofoam® pieces, or precut wood shapes. Then mix up a package of plaster of paris and pour it into a shallow, sturdy box (the lid of a copier paper box is ideal). Have little ones stick their structures into the wet plaster to create a city. Add small pebbles for roads and perhaps a tiny toy car or two. You'll have to work quickly to "cement" everything into place before the plaster hardens. Keep the tiny town on display for classroom visitors to admire!

Family Focus

Invite parents to come to school and build the day away! In advance, collect *lots* of splinter-free wood, nails, sandpaper, wood glue, and assorted tempera paint. Ask parents to bring their own hammers—and their imaginations! Have them work one-on-one with the experienced pros to construct a morning of memories and some interesting souvenirs! Take a break and build some peanut butter and jelly sandwiches. Then have them put the finishing touches on their projects. Take time to show them around the construction site and build their knowledge of what their little ones are learning.

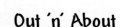

Out 'n' About

Surely there's some construction going on in *your* city or town! Take a class field trip, but this time don't drive by those cranes and bulldozers—make them your destination! Find a safe place for children to watch the action as real construction workers build and create with some of the same tools you've been using at school. Try to arrange for youngsters to interview a worker and be sure to take some photos.

Highlights of Our Trip
At the Construction Site

Caution: Our classroom has been under construction! We've been learning about the planning and hard work it takes to build just about anything—from sidewalks to skycrapers. Here's a blueprint of what we did!

TO TOPSY-TURVY TOWN.

Explore a world of opposites and silliness, where everything is upside down or inside out or just plain *different!* It's a most unexpected adventure!

ADMIT ONE

Getting Ready to Go!
A trip to Topsy-Turvy Town requires packing your bags with some unusual items. Check out the lists on page 67; then gather the supplies you'll need according to the centers you choose. Use the ideas below to help transform your classroom into a place where silly is the standard!

ADMIT ONE

SHAKE THINGS UP

Just before beginning this unit, take some time to rearrange your classroom and move your centers and work tables to new locations. Then go a bit further. Hang center signs, posters, and children's artwork upside down…or sideways…or on the ceiling! Turn all the books on your library center display shelf so that the back covers are facing outward. Spell out the titles on your bulletin boards backwards. Display the alphabet from Z to A, and do any other mixed-up and silly things you can think of!

BACKWARD NAMETAGS

Since your little ones are visitors in Topsy-Turvy Town, they'll need to wear nametags—special, topsy-turvy nametags! To prepare one, take a picture of the back of each child's head; then have the photos developed. Trim each photo and mount it on an index card. Then print the child's name—backwards, of course!—beneath her picture. Have her wear the tag—on her back, of course!

STOCK UP ON SILLY STUFF

Choose from the center ideas on pages 68–73. Here's a handy list of the supplies you'll need to prepare each one.

ART AREA

Color With Your Toes: muffin-tin crayons, butcher paper or newspaper, washable markers (optional)

Unpainting: fingerpainting paper, tempera paint, wooden-handled paintbrushes, combs, spatulas, craft sticks, construction paper

Unsticking: painter's tape, tagboard or cardboard squares, sponges, tempera paint

Unchalking: sidewalk chalk, sponges, construction paper, corrugated cardboard or bubble wrap (optional)

READING CENTER

Stage a Silly Story: props to accompany humorous books (see book list on page 69)

SCIENCE CENTER

Two From One: full-length mirror, variety of small objects

Speaking of Reflections…: makeup mirrors with magnifying sides

Bouncing off the Walls: overhead projector, hand mirrors, colored cellophane strips

MUSIC AND MOVEMENT

Silly Sounds: albums and 45-speed records, record player, cassette tape and recorder

BLOCK AREA

Slinky® Time!: metal Slinky® toys

WRITING CENTER

A World Gone Topsy-Turvy!: chart paper, markers, crayons

SENSORY TABLES AND TUBS

Sticking and Unsticking: soft rubber suction cups, new hand plungers (optional)

Covering and Uncovering: pom-poms, Ping-Pong® balls

Freezing and Unfreezing: gallon-size zippered plastic bags, food coloring, rubber spatulas

Topsy-Turvy Bottles: 16-ounce clear soda bottles with lids, small water-resistant objects, hot glue gun and glue

DRAMATIC-PLAY CENTER

Inside-Out House: cardboard boxes (shoebox size and smaller), hot glue gun and glue, wallpaper samples, fabric scraps, glue, toy cars, dollhouse furniture and accessories

An Unbirthday Party: party plates, cups, napkins, hats, and noisemakers; birthday candles; unbirthday banner; kitchen gadgets

Art Area

Creative expression
Motor skills
Color and texture exploration

COLOR WITH YOUR TOES

How *else* would you color in Topsy-Turvy Town? To make it easier on little toes, create some muffin-tin crayons ahead of time. Just sort a collection of old, broken (unwrapped) crayons into the cups of a mini muffin tin. Then put the tin in a 200-degree oven until the crayons just barely melt. Remove the tin from the oven immediately and allow the new crayons to cool before popping them out. Place large sheets of butcher paper or newspaper on the floor. Have a child slip off his shoes and socks and then use his toes to glide a muffin-tin crayon across the paper. Children can work individually or together—either way, they'll produce a work of art!

For more fun, have youngsters attempt to put washable markers between their toes and draw. Pretty tricky!

UNCHALKING

How do you make chalk drawings without ever touching a stick of chalk to paper? Its easy! Just rub several colors of sidewalk chalk onto damp sponges. Then press the sponges onto art paper. The chalk won't be as dusty, and the inventive shapes and strokes will be a surprise! For more fun, try rubbing chalk onto other damp surfaces, such as corrugated cardboard or bubble wrap.

UNSTICKING

Children *love* to tear and stick! Provide a couple of rolls of painter's tape (available at hardware stores) and some sturdy tagboard or cardboard squares. Have a child tear and stick pieces of tape to her heart's content, pressing the tape onto the board. Then have her sponge tempera paint all over the square. Wait a few minutes; then remove the tape. The one-of-a-kind design will be revealed!

UNPAINTING

Cover a piece of fingerpainting paper (slick side up) with a layer of liquid tempera paint. Then have a young artist use the end of a wooden paintbrush—not the bristles—to draw. Lines will appear instantly! Be creative and try combs, spatulas, or craft sticks, too. Want to save the design? Make a monoprint! (See page 5.)

STAGE A SILLY STORY

What better way to instill a love of reading in children than with laughter and spontaneity? Read some of the humorous stories from the list below; then place the books in your reading area, along with props that help depict silly or unexpected parts of the stories. Your reading area will soon become center stage!

TOPSY-TURVY TALES

Each of these books illustrates the unexpected, the ridiculous, the outlandish, or the not-quite-right. Your little ones will love them all!

If…
By Sarah Perry
Oxford University Press Children's Books

Silly Sally
By Audrey Wood
Harcourt Brace & Company

Cloudy With a Chance of Meatballs
By Judi Barrett
Aladdin Paperbacks

Dogs Don't Wear Sneakers and
Chimps Don't Wear Glasses
Both by Laura Numeroff
Aladdin Paperbacks

To Market, to Market
By Anne Miranda
Harcourt Brace & Company

Just Another Ordinary Day
By Rod Clement
HarperTrophy

Science Center

Analytical thinking
Visual discrimination
Socialization

TWO FROM ONE

In Topsy-Turvy Town, you can't always trust what you see! Create a corner filled with optical interest. Mount a full-length mirror on its side near the floor in your science area. Have a variety of materials with which children can experiment, such as small blocks, combs, pictures or photos cut in half, or playing cards. Ask them to find out what happens when they hold an item in front of a mirror. What about if they slowly touch the edge of an item to the mirror's surface? Is it a match? Is there one or two?

SPEAKING OF REFLECTIONS...

Watch your youngsters come up with the silliest faces ever when you provide makeup mirrors with magnifying sides. Provide mirrors in various sizes and magnifying strengths for lots of discovery and delight!

BOUNCING OFF THE WALLS

Take reflections one step further. Get out the overhead projector, placing it in a clear corner on the floor. Flip on the switch and hand out some handheld mirrors. Then challenge little ones to "bounce" the light off the walls and ceiling. Add some wiggly, giggly color to your light show by supplying colored cellophane strips for youngsters to maneuver on the projector.

Tactile exploration
Language development
Socialization

STICKING AND UNSTICKING

Little ones will really stick to this exploration! Put a small amount of water in a sensory table; then add a variety of soft rubber suction cups. The flexible soap dishes found in the grocery store or the individual round suction cups with plastic hooks are both perfect for this. If you're feeling really adventurous, bring in a couple of brand-new hand plungers, too!

FREEZING AND UNFREEZING

Invite youngsters to help you fill a few gallon-size zippered plastic bags with tinted water. Freeze the bags, allowing them to freeze in whatever shape they happen to take when you wedge them into the freezer. Then peel off the bags and place the frozen shapes into a tub or pool with a few rubber spatulas and start the countdown. Ask children to guess how long it will take for these very unusual ice cubes to melt.

COVERING AND UNCOVERING

Dump a large number of pom-poms (any size or color) into an empty tub or pool. Hide a few Ping-Pong® balls underneath the pom-poms. Children will dig in to find the balls over and over again.

For a wet variation, float a bunch of Ping-Pong® balls in a tub of water; then sink a few colorful pom-poms underneath. Ahh…just the opposite, see?

TOPSY-TURVY BOTTLES

Gather some 16-ounce clear soda bottles. Drop some water-resistant objects—such as crayons, buttons, sequins, or plastic beads—into each one before filling it with water and hot-gluing the cap in place. Then put the bottles next to a tub of water. Invite little ones to see if the bottles sink or float. Ask them to observe the movement of the objects in the bottles. With a shake and a twirl and a flip upside down, they're bound to see the objects do some topsy-turvy tricks!

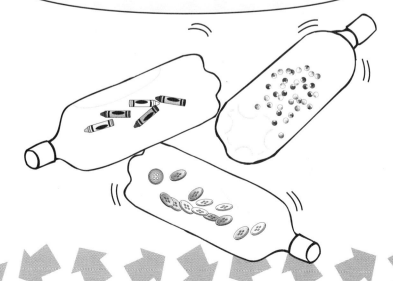

Music and Movement

Auditory skills
Physical coordination
Socialization

SILLY SOUNDS

Here's a use for those outdated albums and 45-speed records. Put them on your record player and play them at nontraditional speeds! Just have youngsters move as the music dictates—superfast or oh-so-slow. Try making a cassette recording of the music, so that children can cue it on their own.

Block Area

Exploration of cause and effect
Collaborative play

SLINKY® TIME!

Remember having *so* much fun with metal Slinky® toys when you were little? These silly toys that move without motors are *still* a hit and easy to find at your local toy or discount store. You'll be amazed at the creative obstacle courses your little ones will come up with when you introduce these toys to your block area!

Writing Center

Creative writing
Language development

A WORLD GONE TOPSY-TURVY!

Have your little ones collaborate to write a report on life in Topsy-Turvy Town. Just ask them to think of things they see in their everyday lives and then imagine what those things are like in this silly place. Grass grows in the sky and everyone walks upside down. Parents serve ice-cream sundaes for breakfast and wear their pajamas to work! Let this get as silly and preposterous as little ones like. Record the report on sheets of chart paper and invite your students to add illustrations, because others might not believe it till they see it!

INSIDE-OUT HOUSE

What if a house were turned inside out? Would the family car be parked inside? Would the kitchen be in the front yard? Would the dishes be hung out on the line to dry? Would there be a flower garden in the bathtub? Invite little ones to explore this idea with a homemade dollhouse. Make one by hot-gluing a number of boxes together to make rooms. Provide wallpaper samples and fabric scraps for outdoor wallpaper and curtains. Have a toy car or two and some dollhouse furniture and accessories for youngsters to manipulate.

Happy Unbirthday to You!

AN UNBIRTHDAY PARTY

In Topsy-Turvy Town, they don't celebrate birthdays. They celebrate unbirthdays instead! So any day that's *not* your birthday is a day for a party! Provide youngsters with all the makings of an unbirthday party, such as party plates, cups, napkins, candles, hats, and noisemakers. Hang a banner that reads "Happy Unbirthday to You!" and supply the kitchen tools to make an unbirthday cake. Hmmm…wonder what's in one of *those*?

TIPS FOR AN EXTENDED STAY

After filling your classroom centers with the wild and wacky, try these ideas for group silliness, outdoor exploration, and family involvement.

ALL TOGETHER NOW

Involve your youngsters in making this display to show off your topsy-turvy travels. First, have each child pose for a photograph with her arms up and her palms flat toward the ceiling (as if she were performing a handstand if she were upside down). Have the photos developed; then carefully cut around each child's body. Mount the cutout photos on a sheet of poster board *upside down*, so it appears that each child is standing on her hands. Add the title "Everything's Topsy-Turvy in [Teacher's name]'s Room!" Post the poster on your door; then invite curious visitors to step inside and take a look around!

Everything's
Topsy-Turvy
in
Mrs. Jones's Room!

OUT 'N' ABOUT

Take the concepts of *in* and *out*, *over* and *under*, and *up* and *down* onto your playground. Provide rolls of landscaping border tape (available in hardware stores) and watch the outdoor art appear as your youngsters weave ribbons of color all over your playground equipment! Just tie the loose end of a roll of tape to a piece of equipment, and then have a youngster hold onto the roll and let it unwind as he climbs up the slide and then slides down, or climbs up the jungle gym and then back down again. Little ones can undo their art by retracing their play in the opposite direction, winding up the tape as they go.

FAMILY FOCUS

Declare a Topsy-Turvy Day at school! Invite children to come to school wearing their clothing backwards or inside out. Ask parents to pick up their little ones a bit early. Then invite them in for a topsy-turvy treat—upside-down ice-cream cones! Serve each child and guest a scoop of ice cream in a disposable bowl with the cone on top. Just for fun, provide plastic forks, instead of spoons, to eat these creations.

HIGHLIGHTS OF OUR TRIP
TOPSY-TURVY TOWN

We've just returned from a wacky world. Read below to find out what we did!

75

Over in the Meadow

Butterfly wings and squiggly things...find out what joys the meadow brings! There are lots of tiny treasures hiding in a meadow, so invite your little ones on a meadow exploration.

Getting Ready to Go!

Prepare for this journey to the marvelous meadow by packing a few supplies. Check out the lists on page 77; then gather what you'll need according to the centers you choose. Use the ideas below to further set the meadow mood in your classroom.

ADMIT ONE

ADMIT ONE

The Big Sky

How can you bring the wonder of the vast outdoors inside? Try creating a whimsical sky made from panels of blue netting either draped from your ceiling or tacked to a wall or two. Cut clouds from foam board or poster board, and then hang them with fishing line or ribbon.

Peeking Into Puddles

Splash a few puddles around the room. Cut puddle shapes from blue construction paper (or Con-Tact® paper). Adhere these to your floor with clear Con-Tact paper. Cut out some frogs and turtles from magazines or clip art and use clear Con-Tact paper to stick these to the floor as well.

Perfect Props

Simple props—such as picnic baskets, quilts, straw hats, rubber boots, and butterfly nets—will invite children to enjoy a wonderful day in your classroom meadow. Collect some stuffed animals to be special meadow friends during this unit, too.

eadow Materials

Choose from the center ideas on pages 78–83. Here's a handy list of the supplies you'll need to prepare each one.

Art Area

Flying Meadow Bugs: small Styrofoam® plates, construction paper, tissue paper, sequins, glue, chenille stems, string, canning lid rings

Spidery Webs: dental floss, Styrofoam® plates or trays, plastic sewing needles

Beeswax Delight: beeswax, white construction paper, blue and green food coloring, paintbrushes

Birds' Nests: clay or homemade modeling dough, straw, yarn, shredded paper, birdseed, disposable bowls, plastic eggs

Reading Center

A Quiet Place to Read: green blanket or sheet, blue throw rug, stuffed animals, quilt or blanket, picnic basket

Science Center

Guess Who!: cassette player and tape

Dramatic-Play Center

Buzz on Over!: pictures of flowers, silk flowers, T-shirts painted with black and yellow stripes, plastic headbands, pipe cleaners, pom-poms, hot glue gun and glue, streamers, wooden bowls, kitchen utensils

Writing Center

A Rhythmic Story: chart paper, markers

Crawling, Flying Stories: caterpillar- and butterfly-shaped blank books, watercolors, thick and thin markers

Music and Movement

Meadow Movement: instrumental recordings with a nature theme, sheer scarves, glasses or glass bottles, water, spoons

Block Area

Burrow With the Bunnies: large box, brown "plue" (see page 4), green Easter grass, stuffed rabbits, pillows, blanket

Ants Aplenty: laundry basket

Sensory Tables and Tubs

Fishin' for Gold: small orange and yellow balloons, aquarium fishnets or small sieves, blue and green food coloring, hook-free fishing lures

The Search Is On!: quick-sprouting grass seed, potting soil, sheet of plastic, plastic or rubber insects, magnifying glasses, tweezers

Skipping Stones: blue food coloring, clean pebbles and small stones, slotted spoons, colanders

Bits of Sparkling Sunlight: green and gold sequins, green food coloring, wooden spoons, aquarium fishnets

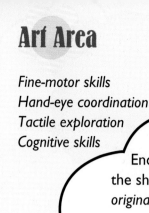

Art Area

Fine-motor skills
Hand-eye coordination
Tactile exploration
Cognitive skills

Flying Meadow Bugs

Encourage each of your young artists to create a kite in the shape of a ladybug, a beetle, a bumblebee, or a new *original* bug! Simply provide Styrofoam® plates, and an assortment of construction paper, tissue paper, and sequins, along with an ample supply of school glue. Add chenille stems that can be poked through plates to make legs and antennae. To attach kite strings, poke two holes in the center of each plate; then thread a long length of string through both holes and tie it in place. Then head outdoors and try running with these fliers in tow! Afterward, hang them from your classroom ceiling.

Spidery Webs

Weave some wonderful webs with dental floss! To prepare one, cut the center from a Styrofoam® plate or tray. Then thread a length of dental floss through a plastic sewing needle. Have a child randomly poke the needle through the Styrofoam frame, crisscrossing the floss in a tangled web design. Help the child tie the loose end of the floss and remove the needle. Hang these around your classroom-turned-meadow or outdoors on a tree for all to see.

Beeswax Delight

Beeswax can be purchased in most craft supply stores and smells as delicious as it feels! Give each child a small amount of wax to work with. (The warmth of a child's hands will make the wax soft and pliable.) After she's explored for a while, have each youngster use the wax to color an invisible picture on white construction paper. Then have her "paint" over her picture with lovely blue and green meadow colors. A few drops of food coloring added to water is the perfect "paint" for this wax-resist technique.

Birds' Nests

It's fun to find a real bird's nest, but you can also make one of your own! Give each of your bird lovers a ball of clay or your favorite homemade modeling dough. Provide straw, bits and pieces of colorful yarn, shredded paper, and birdseed. Have each child knead some of the materials into his clay and then shape the nest and let it rest in a disposable bowl. For a fun surprise, nestle a plastic egg inside each clay nest when little ones are out of the room.

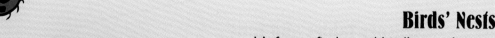

A Quiet Place to Read

Spread a big green blanket or sheet on the floor in your reading area and you'll have flowing fields of grass. Add a blue throw rug pond and invite some special furry friends from your stuffed animal collection to an indoor-outdoor storytime! Spread a quilt or blanket and add a picnic basket full of good books. Then watch little ones lie back and enjoy a story or two!

Meadow Reading

Youngsters will enjoy these books about meadows and the creatures that live there.

In the Tall, Tall Grass
By Denise Fleming
Henry Holt and Company

The Very Hungry Caterpillar
By Eric Carle
The Putnam Publishing Group

The Very Quiet Cricket: A Multisensory Book
By Eric Carle
Philomel Books

Over in the Meadow: An Old Nursery Counting Rhyme
By Paul Galdone
Simon & Schuster

One Duck Stuck
By Phyllis Root
Candlewick Press

Pond
By Lizi Boyd
Chronicle Books

Writing Center

Language development
Word association
Listening skills
Writing skills

quack quack

A Rhythmic Story

Quack, chirp, and ribbit your way through this fun group story! Teach little ones the rhyme below. Then invite each child to choose an animal and its sound to fill in the blanks. Record the rhyme and the children's choices on a big sheet of chart paper. Invite them to illustrate it when it's complete.

Over in the meadow on a very sunny day,
I spotted a/an [animal] and it began to say, "[animal's sound]."

Over in the meadow on a very sunny day,
I spotted a bee and it began to say, "Buzz, buzz."

Over in the meadow on a very sunny day,
I spotted a frog and it began to say, "Ribbit, ribbit."

Over in the meadow on a very sunny day,
I spotted a cricket and it began to say, "Chirp, chirp."

The catrplr goe to a Kakn.

Crawling, Flying Stories

Cut writing paper and construction paper into the shapes of caterpillars and butterflies. Put together shaped books with construction paper covers for your young authors; then invite them to create their own tales about creepy caterpillars and fluttering butterflies. Supply watercolors, as well as thick and thin markers for illustrating.

This catrplr is hungre. He will et 80 LEVZ.

Motor skills
Exploration of cause and effect
Counting
Socialization

Fishin' for Gold

Create your own private fishpond in a baby pool by adding lots of goldfish—the kind made from small orange and yellow water balloons! Provide aquarium fishnets or small sieves for easy fishing. To make the water a dreamy shade of teal, add a couple of drops of blue and green food coloring. For a wiggly treat, add hook-free fishing lures, found in the fishing section of sporting goods stores.

The Search Is On!

Grow a minimeadow right in your classroom! Add some quick-sprouting grass seed to a sensory table or tub full of potting soil. Sprinkle on some water and leave the tub covered with a sheet of plastic over a weekend. You'll have a surprise on Monday morning! When the grass grows tall enough, hide some plastic or rubber insects in it. Provide magnifying glasses and challenge little ones to find the creepy-crawlies. Tweezers make great bug picker-uppers!

Skipping Stones

Your classroom doesn't have *quite* as much space as the great outdoors, but youngsters can still search for the perfect pebble or stone to toss in the water and then count the ripples! Fill a shallow baby pool with lightly tinted water. Sink a variety of clean pebbles and small stones purchased from the garden section of your local home improvement store or nursery. Provide slotted spoons and colanders to help little ones sift through their discoveries. They'll enjoy digging up the pebbles and tossing them back in again and again.

Bits of Sparkling Sunlight

Create the effect of a summer pond, glistening with sunlight. Sprinkle several small bags of green and gold sequins into a pool or tub of water tinted light green. Add wooden spoons and aquarium fishnets for stirring and scooping bits of sunlight!

Dramatic-Play Center

Creative play
Language development
Socialization

Buzz on Over!

Transform your dramatic-play area into a busy, buzzing beehive! Cut out and laminate lots of pictures of flowers and display them all around the center. Add some silk flowers, too. To help your little ones dress the part of bees, provide large T-shirts painted with black and yellow stripes. Bend some pipe cleaners around inexpensive headbands and hot-glue pom-poms to the top of these fashionable antennae. Designate one chair as the queen bee's throne and have worker bees decorate it with streamers and flowers. Of course, you'll need some big wooden bowls and some kitchen utensils for making honey!

Music and Movement

Auditory skills
Motor skills
Rhythm
Socialization

Meadow Movement

Check out some nature-themed instrumental recordings from your local library. Provide a box of sheer scarves for windy and watery movement exploration. If you can provide supervision, set up glasses or glass bottles with varying amounts of water. Add some spoons and encourage little ones to create their own meadow melodies.

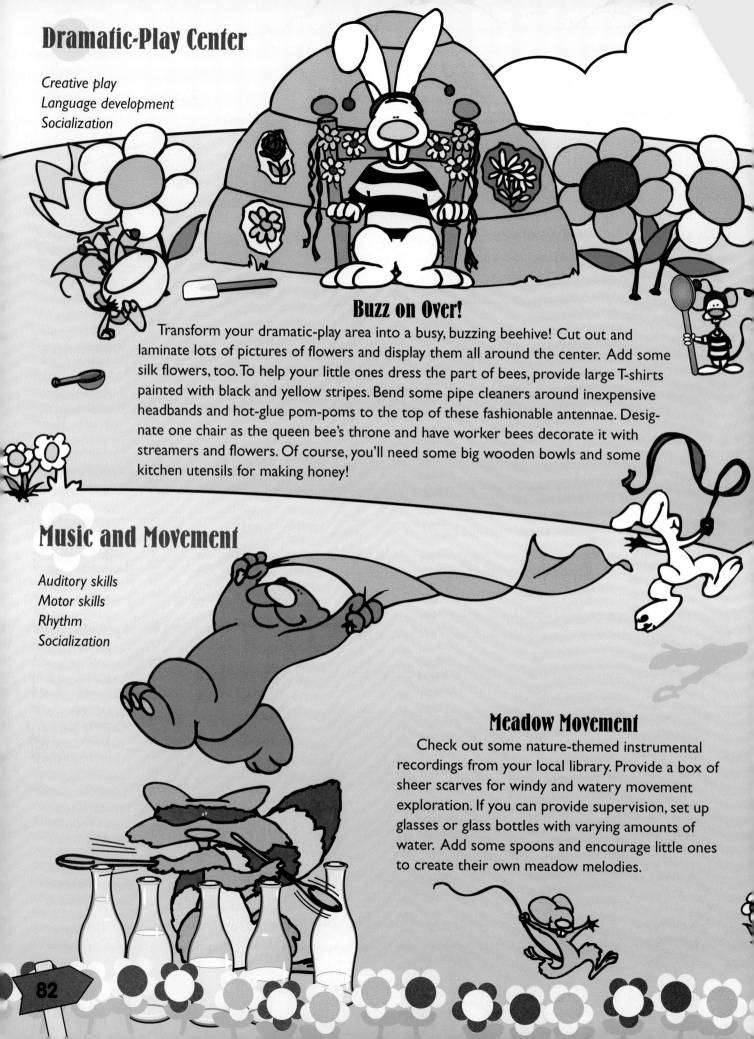

Science Center

Auditory skills
Cognitive skills
Memory recall

Guess Who!

Liven up your science area with a meadow guessing game! Invite the children to join you in making a cassette tape of animal sounds and clues about different creatures that might be found in a meadow. For example, say into the tape recorder, "I have feathers and webbed feet. I say...." Then have children provide the quacking sounds. Finish up the clue by saying, "Can you guess who I am?" After recording each clue, leave a pause for little ones to guess. Place the tape and tape recorder in your science center and teach youngsters how to play and rewind the tape.

Block Area

Collaborative play
Motor skills
Cognitive skills

Burrow With the Bunnies

What would it be like to live in a rabbit's den? Youngsters can explore this idea with a few props in your block area. Turn a large box into a cozy underground nest by using brown-tinted "plue" (see page 4) to adhere green Easter grass all over the outside. Fit the grass-covered box into a corner of your block center; then add a few snuggly stuffed bunnies, some soft pillows, and a toasty blanket to make a rabbit hideaway.

Ants Aplenty

In every lush, green meadow, there are countless ants busily tunneling below the ground. Your block area can become a busy anthill in no time. Flip over a laundry basket (call it an *anthill starter,* if you will) and then watch your worker ants get busy building all around it—any way they choose! You'll see pathways and tunnels galore in no time!

Tips for an Extended Stay

Once you've transformed your classroom centers into a lush meadow, try these ideas to extend your theme into a group activity, outdoor fun, and a family project.

All Together Now

Make a gigantic class caterpillar to decorate classroom walls. Provide lots of small paper plates, a variety of tissue paper pieces, paintbrushes, and some liquid starch to use as "invisible paint." Encourage everyone to decorate as many plates as they'd like. (Each child can take one or two home, and your caterpillar will still be a healthy size!) Staple the plates together, or punch holes on opposite sides of each plate and connect them with pipe cleaner pieces for a more fluid look.

Out 'n' About

Plan a Caterpillar Hunt on your playground! First, mold small caterpillars (a class supply or more) from play dough. Place each one inside a plastic egg—so it's ready to hatch, of course—and then hide all the eggs in the meadow (your outdoor play area). Take little ones outdoors and invite them to find and hide these hatching critters over and over. When the fun's done, invite each child to take a meadow friend home to keep.

Family Focus

Even preschool parents and children can have home-work sometimes! Suggest that parents take their youngsters for a nature walk and then send to school at least three items they've found. These don't have to be items from a meadow—any outdoor walk is fine. Encourage little ones to share their treasures with the class.

Highlights of Our Trip
Over in the Meadow

Creatures that flutter and fly—oh, my! We met all kinds of friendly critters on our trip to the marvelous meadow. Read on to find out all about it!

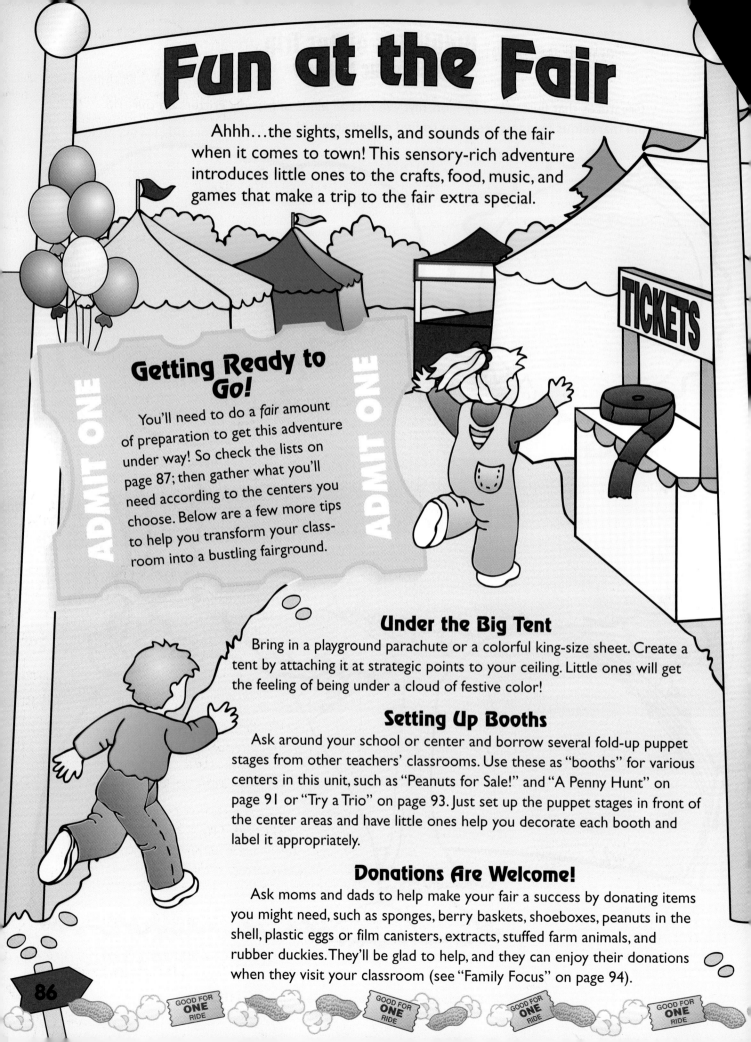

Fun at the Fair

Ahhh…the sights, smells, and sounds of the fair when it comes to town! This sensory-rich adventure introduces little ones to the crafts, food, music, and games that make a trip to the fair extra special.

Getting Ready to Go!

You'll need to do a *fair* amount of preparation to get this adventure under way! So check the lists on page 87; then gather what you'll need according to the centers you choose. Below are a few more tips to help you transform your classroom into a bustling fairground.

Under the Big Tent

Bring in a playground parachute or a colorful king-size sheet. Create a tent by attaching it at strategic points to your ceiling. Little ones will get the feeling of being under a cloud of festive color!

Setting Up Booths

Ask around your school or center and borrow several fold-up puppet stages from other teachers' classrooms. Use these as "booths" for various centers in this unit, such as "Peanuts for Sale!" and "A Penny Hunt" on page 91 or "Try a Trio" on page 93. Just set up the puppet stages in front of the center areas and have little ones help you decorate each booth and label it appropriately.

Donations Are Welcome!

Ask moms and dads to help make your fair a success by donating items you might need, such as sponges, berry baskets, shoeboxes, peanuts in the shell, plastic eggs or film canisters, extracts, stuffed farm animals, and rubber duckies. They'll be glad to help, and they can enjoy their donations when they visit your classroom (see "Family Focus" on page 94).

GOOD FOR ONE RIDE GOOD FOR ONE RIDE GOOD FOR ONE RIDE GOOD FOR ONE RIDE

Fair Furnishings

Choose from the center ideas on pages 88–93. Here's a handy list of the supplies you'll need to prepare each one.

Science Center

Something Smells Yummy!: extracts, cotton balls, jars, index cards, marker, tape

Art Area

Quick 'n' Crazy Shape Quilts: quilt or pictures of quilts, muslin or cotton fabric squares, fabric paint, shallow trays, sponge shapes, construction paper strips or sewing machine

Balloon Painting: flour, helium-quality balloons, funnel, string, tempera paint, muffin tin, easel paper

Free-Form Basket Weaving: berry baskets, materials for weaving

A Day at the Fair: shoebox lids, glue, collage materials to represent the fair

Dramatic-Play Center

Clownin' Around: dress-up clothing, trunk or suitcase, mirrors, face paint (optional), disposable cameras (optional)

Pick a Prize: water table, rubber duckies, permanent marker, typical fair prizes

Music and Movement

Local Sounds: recordings of regional music, rhythm instruments

Reading Center

Books in the Barn: bales of hay, stuffed farm animals, buckets, theme-related books

Block Area

Try a Trio: wooden blocks, Con-Tact® paper, tagboard squares, scissors, marker

Constructing the Fairgrounds: large piece of felt or strips of masking tape, wooden blocks, DUPLO® blocks, people and farm animal figures, toy cars and trucks

Sensory Tables and Tubs

Peanuts for Sale!: unshelled peanuts or Styrofoam® peanuts, brown paper lunch bags, scoops, simple scale

Bobbin' for Oranges: oranges, ice-cream scoops or tongs, large bowl, towels

"Cotton-y" Candy: pink tempera paint, spray bottle, polyester fiberfill, large bowls, plastic salad tongs, pasta forks

A Penny Hunt: large quantity of plastic eggs or film canisters decorated with stickers, a few pennies, hot glue gun and glue, slotted spoons, bowls, blindfolds (optional)

Writing Center

Ready to Ride!: construction paper, crayons, marker, staples or other binding

GOOD FOR ONE RIDE

GOOD FOR ONE RIDE

GOOD FOR ONE RIDE

GOOD FOR ONE RIDE

Art Area

Color and shape recognition
Sequencing
Patterning
Fine-motor skills
Creativity

Arts & Crafts

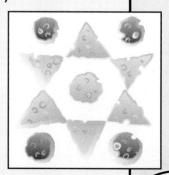

Balloon Painting

Here's a fun new way to paint at the easel! Flour-filled balloons make squishy-squashy and wonderful painting tools! Just use a funnel to fill small, helium-quality balloons with flour; then tie them closed and wipe them off with a damp cloth. Squirt a few colors of tempera paint into the cups of a muffin tin and place a balloon in each one. Invite young artists to paint and print with these squeezable balloons as they invent an assortment of shapes and colors at your easel!

Quick 'n' Crazy Shape Quilts

Little ones can create blue-ribbon quilts with fabric paint and an array of sponge shapes. Show your class a quilt or some pictures of quilts. Ask them to identify the various shapes they see. Then give each child a square of inexpensive muslin or cotton fabric. Supply basic shapes cut from sponges and shallow trays of fabric paint. Have each quilter dip sponges into fabric paint and then onto her square, creating a pattern as she desires. Allow the paint to dry overnight, and follow any other instructions given on the bottle for setting the paint. If you're handy with a sewing machine, you can actually sew the squares together to create a quilt. Otherwise, attach the squares to a bulletin board and add construction paper strips between them.

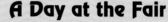

A Day at the Fair

Invite each child to take a piece of your classroom fair home when he makes a box collage. Give each child a shoebox lid and glue. Then supply a sampling of fair reminders: popped popcorn, real peanut shells or Styrofoam® peanuts, die-cut balloon shapes, construction paper triangles (to represent tents), and maybe some pink cotton balls to play the part of prize pigs! Check out the materials in your classroom centers and you may come up with other good ideas. Allow youngsters to revisit these projects and keep adding to them for a few days if they choose.

GOOD FOR ONE RIDE
GOOD FOR ONE RIDE
GOOD FOR ONE RIDE
GOOD FOR ONE RIDE

Books in the Barn

Transform your book nook into a cozy barn where little ones can read stories to all the prizewinning livestock (the soft, stuffed kind). Bring in a couple of bales of hay and lots of stuffed animals like those you might see at a fair—sheep, cows, pigs, and horses. And since the animals at *this* fair like to munch on a good story, put some theme-related books in "feed buckets" and set them in the center.

A Fair Selection

Your students will want to step right up and listen to these stories about the fair!

Carousel
By Brian Wildsmith
Oxford University Press
    Children's Books

Night at the Fair
By Donald Crews
Greenwillow Books

Going to the Fair
By Sheryl MacFarlane
Orca Book Publishers

Come to the Fair
By Janet Lunn
Tundra Books

Grandma's Smile
By Elaine Moore
Lothrop, Lee &
    Shepard Books

GOOD FOR ONE RIDE
GOOD FOR ONE RIDE
GOOD FOR ONE RIDE
GOOD FOR ONE RIDE

Dramatic-Play Center

Creative thinking
Collaborative play
Language development
Numeral recognition and matching

Clownin' Around

No fair would be complete without clowns! Pack all kinds of dress-up clothing in an old trunk or suitcase and your housekeeping area will soon be a main attraction! Big shoes, silly wigs, hats, gloves, colorful neckties, suspenders, and vests all make great clown gear. Be sure to have plenty of mirrors on hand, so little ones can see themselves. Real face paint and some disposable cameras are added touches that will make this center extra fun!

Pick a Prize

This center features a booth where everyone wins and children give and get the prizes again and again! Bring over a water table and partially fill it with water. Use a permanent marker to write a different number on the bottom of each of several rubber duckies. Float the duckies in the water. Then gather an equal number of prizes that are typical of a fair, such as stuffed animals, inflatable balls, plastic jewelry, or toy cars. Display the prizes, each with a number that matches a duckie, on a table. Children who visit this center take turns being the patrons (who pick the rubber duckies) and "running" the booth (matching the duckie's number to a prize and giving it away).

GOOD FOR **ONE** RIDE GOOD FOR **ONE** RIDE GOOD FOR **ONE** RIDE GOOD FOR **ONE** RIDE

Sensory Tables and Tubs

Tactile exploration
Fine-motor skills
Size and weight comparison
Collaborative play

Peanuts for Sale!

What would a fair be without mounds of peanuts in the shell? Help youngsters run their own peanut booth by filling a sensory table with unshelled peanuts. Add some scoops, brown paper lunch bags, and a simple scale. If you have students with peanut allergies, substitute Styrofoam® peanuts—it'll be just as fun!

Bobbin' for Oranges

Oranges? Yes! They can withstand a lot more bobbing than apples and *still* be good for a snack. Have children use ice-cream scoops or tongs instead of their mouths to catch oranges floating in a tub of water. (This takes *lots* of coordination!) Place a big bowl nearby for holding the oranges little ones manage to retrieve. Also have a few towels on hand for wiping up drips.

"Cotton-y" Candy

Make some fake cotton candy that's just as fun (but not as tasty) as the real thing. Lightly spray pink tempera paint onto polyester fiberfill. Allow it to dry; then put the pinkish fluff in a sensory table, along with big bowls, plastic salad tongs, and some pasta forks.

A Penny Hunt

Who can resist a treasure hunt— even if the prize is only a pretty penny? Bring out enough plastic eggs (or film canisters decorated with colorful stickers) to fill a sensory table. Then tuck a penny into just a few eggs, sealing each one with hot glue to secure it. Provide some slotted spoons and bowls to help little ones sort. When a child finds an egg with a penny inside, he returns it to the pool for others to find. For an added challenge, offer blindfolds to the hunters!

Science Center

Analytical thinking
Word association
Sensory experience

Music and Movement

Rhythm
Physical coordination
Socialization

Something Smells Yummy!

Invite your students to identify some of the delicious smells one might find at a fair. Put a few drops of an extract—such as strawberry, lemon, orange, peppermint, or root beer—on a cotton ball. Then tuck the cotton ball inside a labeled jar. Use the leftover extract to add a sensory delight to paint or homemade play dough.

Local Sounds

What kind of music is featured at fairs in your region? Would youngsters hear fiddles and banjos? Brass bands? Accordion music? Whatever it might be, find some musical recordings or, better yet, some live musicians to share their talents with your students! Pass out the rhythm instruments and invite little ones to play along. Then have them move to the beat, whether it's fast, slow, or somewhere in between.

Writing Center

Word association
Vocabulary development
Writing skills

Ready to Ride!

What's *your* favorite ride at the fair? Do you like the rush of the roller coaster or the slower pace of the carousel? Riding high on a Ferris wheel or bouncing around in the bumper cars? Ask each child to illustrate her favorite fair ride and dictate why she likes it best. Bind the pages together into a class book with the title "We're Ready to Ride!"

GOOD FOR ONE RIDE

GOOD FOR ONE RIDE

GOOD FOR ONE RIDE

GOOD FOR ONE RIDE

Try a Trio

Use the blocks in your block center for this matching game for one or more players. To prepare it, select about two dozen blocks in different sizes and shapes. Trace each block onto solid-colored Con-Tact® paper twice and cut out the shapes. Adhere one cutout to the block and the other to a tagboard square to create a matching card. Place all the cards facedown. When a "contestant" chooses a card, she finds the matching block and places it atop the card. When all the cards have matching blocks, remove them, mix up the cards, and begin again. Children will be matching colors, shapes, and sizes all at once!

Constructing the Fairgrounds

Encourage little builders to construct a miniature fairground in your block center. Put down a large piece of felt or just outline the grounds with masking tape borders. Then provide wooden blocks, DUPLO® blocks, people figures, farm animal figures, and toy cars and trucks. Allow this creative construction to continue for several days, as youngsters learn more about the fair and want to add more details.

Tips for an Extended Stay

When your classroom centers are "fair-ly" well prepared, consider these ideas for a group activity, outdoor fun, and parent involvement.

All Together Now

Apples, anyone? Have little ones help you prepare a festive treat of candied or caramel apples. Follow your favorite recipe and encourage youngsters to help with all the steps they can, such as washing the apples, inserting the craft sticks, and measuring the ingredients for the coating. This will be such a hit, you'll want to make extras to share!

Out 'n' About

Here's a new kind of fair "ride" your youngsters will love! Set up an obstacle course for riding toys on a hard surface. Use plastic cones or laundry baskets in strategic spots; then designate the path with ribbon or thin rope. Post directional arrows to point little riders the right way, as well as a sign at the end that says "You Did It!" Children can walk, skip, hop, or gallop the trail while waiting for a turn on a riding toy.

Family Focus

Have a Fun Fair Day and invite parents to come to your classroom to participate in the games, crafts, and other activities in this unit. Hand out free tickets at the door, as well as maps of your fairgrounds with each center activity listed. The experienced fairgoers (your students) will be glad to show moms and dads around! Serve some ice-cold pink lemonade or root beer to top off this special day!

Highlights of Our Trip
Fun at the Fair

Ahhh…the smell of cotton candy! The games! The music! The excitement!
We had our very own fair at school. So step right up and read all about it!

Plan Your Own Classroom Adventure!

Destination: _____

Art Area

Reading Center

Dramatic-Play Center

Science Center

Sensory Tables and Tubs

Block Area

Writing Center

Music and Movement

Tips for an Extended Stay:

FUN—2 mi.